# Are you an overdependent child— even as an adult?

- Although you're successful in some areas of your life, you still feel as though you haven't been able to move forward in other areas on your own.
- You're in a great job, but you have difficulty developing relationships.
- Your parents' way of doing things dictates how you think you and your spouse should operate.
- You often feel your parents are trying to tell you how to raise your child.

## Are you an overinvolved parent?

- You insist that your four-year-old eat everything on his or her plate.
- You constantly remind your ten-year-old to wear a coat on a cold day.
- You let your child sleep with you and your spouse regularly, rather than in a bed of his or her own.
- You rarely leave your child to be taken care of by other people.

IF ANY OF THESE APPLY TO YOU, YOU'RE NOT ALONE. *MOTHERS WHO LOVE TOO MUCH* CAN HELP YOU TURN THESE POTENTIALLY DESTRUCTIVE BEHAVIOR PATTERNS INTO A MORE HEALTHFUL, BALANCED LOVE.

# MOTHERS WHO LOVE TOO MUCH

## Breaking Dependent Love Patterns in Family Relationships

### Anne F. Grizzle
### with William Proctor

Previously entitled:
MOTHER LOVE, MOTHER HATE

IVY BOOKS • NEW YORK

*To my mother, Helen Fletcher,*
*for years of faithful enabling love*

Ivy Books
Published by Ballantine Books
Copyright © 1988 by Anne F. Grizzle and William Proctor

Library of Congress Catalog Card Number: 87-91505

ISBN 0-8041-0588-X

Manufactured in the United States of America

First Hardcover Edition: September 1988
First Mass Market Edition: May 1991

# Contents

# Acknowledgments

A child grows to adulthood through the nurturing of not only his mother and father but a whole host of family members. In a similar vein, while I am the obvious mother of this book, its ideas have been nurtured to final form through the efforts of many people.

My interest in families and perspective of people, not as isolated individuals but as persons in relationships, stems in large part from the warmth and depth of my own family relationships. I am especially thankful to my mother and father who gave me abundant love coupled with encouragement to try new challenges. They, as well as my grandparents, sisters, aunts, and uncles introduced me to the intricacies of families: celebrated traditions, unspoken rules, repeating patterns, and the thickness of blood. My husband, David, has helped me discover personally the rewards and challenges of blending two family styles to create a new family. My two sons, Benjamin and Joshua, have given me great daily joy as a mother even as they test my own ability to practice enabling love.

I first learned about family systems therapy, the underlying perspective of this book, from Regina Kohn at Columbia University, to whom I am grateful for continued support. My systemic focus was further honed by advanced training with the family therapy faculty at Hunter College School of Social Work. Dr. Sonya Rhodes, as supervisor and mentor, enthusiastically supported me in turning professional understandings into a book.

For the original impetus to write *Mothers Who Love Too Much* and for introducing me to the practical process of writing a book I am indebted to Bill Proctor. Joëlle

Delbourgo, through her enabling editing style, encouraged both quality and genuineness in the writing. For personal encouragement in this project, I am especially thankful to Mark Campisano, ever ready supporter and helpful critic. Also thanks to Beth Fletcher, Laura Henry, Diane Sherwood, Betsy Smylie, and Kathy Wiegand.

Finally, my thanks to all the families who have entrusted their problems and relationships to me in counseling. They are the ones who have best taught me the strengths of devoted families, the possibilities for change and the rewards of the growth process.

# Preface

Yesterday, my six-year-old son wrote me "a love song" that almost brought me to tears. Four hours later, after a disagreement, he shouted angrily, "I hate you!" As adults, we usually express our feelings less directly than this but we feel them no less intensely. Often we feel most deeply hurt by the people we most deeply love. So our strongest feelings—both love and hate—are usually reserved for the people closest to us. For most of us, our first intimate relationship is with our mother. And whether we are six or sixty, whether we see our mother every day or every four years, our feelings often remain intense.

As a family therapist, I encounter people wrestling with the duality of mother love, mother hate daily. A middle-aged woman, who had lived a continent away from her family for four years, sought my help for serious physical problems brought on by her intense connection and conflict with her mother. A twenty-eight-year-old man came to see me because he felt tremendous guilt about moving out of the apartment he shared with his mother to live with a friend. A very dependent teenager with an eating disorder complained that if only her mother would leave her alone, everything in her life would be fine. In each of these cases, I was presented with a conflict between a child and mother. However, in exploring each situation more fully, I discovered that the love-hate feelings between mother and child were just one part of a much broader family pattern of interaction—a pattern that I call the Dependent Love Pattern.

These three individuals and their families, and those like them who seek my help, are actually among the emotionally strongest people I see. They are not victims of abuse and neglect, like those whose stories appear in our daily newspapers. They come from families who care very deeply. These adult children do not easily dismiss their parents nor do their parents write them off as irresponsible. Many, though troubled, are often highly successful. They may be grappling with serious problems, but they also bring with them a vital core of strength. That core is their intense caring involvement, which gives them the energy to continue wrestling with each other, working to find a way to express their love without producing hate.

Even the strongest families have conflicts and difficulties. I see dedicated parents who are deeply troubled over their children's problems. I see children who are devoted to their parents but who are frustrated and thwarted in their own careers or relationships. I see families with strong faith who are committed to one another but who clash repeatedly. It is a privilege for me to help these families—they have the important foundation of commitment and love. Helping them learn how to love each other more wisely is so much easier than helping a family learn how to love at all!

I have written *Mothers Who Love Too Much* for people who come from committed, caring families and who wish to prevent problems, or who find they currently have problems that they can't resolve. I hope to affirm the very real strengths of these families while enabling them to recognize and change potentially destructive patterns of behavior that can produce hostility, and eventually even hatred, within the closest families. I prefer prevention to intervention—helping families to correct imbalances before they escalate into crises.

My training and experience has led me to believe more and more strongly in the importance of considering the entire system of family relationships in order to resolve the problems of even one person. While the last twenty-five years have seen a remarkable growth in the knowledge of family systems in professional circles, the public at large has yet to benefit from this. In this book, I will share some of that wealth of family understanding with you. As you read, I hope that you will be able to begin to understand better how your own family works and to try new approaches for healing and growth.

In *Mothers Who Love Too Much* I will share the experiences of those who have sought my help to correct the imbalances in their families. The names and certain facts have been changed to protect confidentiality; but the situations that I describe are real ones. I hope the experiences of these families who have worked hard for change will give you courage to explore new avenues for better relationships within your own family.

When you are experiencing great hurt and anger, it takes a lot of energy to work toward positive relationships, rather than just giving up or blaming others. It also takes humility and caring to work at the understanding and healing process when you do not see yourself as having a problem. Yet I see many family members who are willing to do just that—and I enjoy seeing them reap the rewards of their effort. So I hope that as you read this book and examine your own family patterns and your part in them, you, too, will find your efforts at understanding and change producing great rewards. My goal is to help people move beyond entrapping, angering family relationships, toward enjoyable, respectful adult relationships with the family members they love.

*Anne F. Grizzle*

# Part I

MOTHER LOVE,
MOTHER HATE

# Chapter 1

---

# THE LOVE—HATE RELATIONSHIP BETWEEN MOTHER AND CHILD

*"Deep down, I know I really love my mother. I mean, she's done so much for me. She's the one person who's always there for me. She cooks, she'll watch the children on a moment's notice, and she's got advice for every situation. Although we both need to talk, we often scream at each other. Sometimes, I even hate her. Nobody can get me so mad and crazy. My husband has complained that I'm married to her instead of to him! Sometimes, though, I just can't stand her anymore and I wish she'd leave me alone!"*
—*An adult child*

*"I've devoted my life to being a good mother. I've done everything possible for my son. I've really given my all. But something's gone terribly wrong: He complains all the time. He doesn't do a thing at home. And now, he's having some awful emotional problem. I don't understand, and I don't know what else I can do to help."*

—*A mother*

How can a daughter, who knows she is greatly loved by her mother, feel so oppressed at times that she genuinely hates her?

And how can a mother, who has loved so much, have an adult child who is still an emotional infant?

Over and over, people bring these questions to me in my office. These are wonderful, interesting, and often extremely successful people who *know* they're loved and that they belong! They are caring, sensitive, and concerned children and parents.

Yet these loved and loving people are struggling with very real and even crippling problems. Their problems may not be as glaring as those of some people, but they may well be more costly. I say costly because their capacity to understand and give love may be greater than that of many other individuals, but their talents and their generous natures may be locked in or thwarted.

What's the explanation for this paradox? The answer, I believe, lies in a family pattern I've observed in which necessary, caring love isn't balanced by the encouragement of independence. Sometimes, nurturing, giving love can be distorted into a clutching possessiveness, a concern that won't let go. Natural caring becomes fearful overprotectiveness. Doing for a child replaces teaching a child to do for himself or herself. Consequently, the youngster becomes "smothered" by excessive care. He or she becomes a captive—and lacks the freedom to grow up completely.

This distorted love, which becomes a disabling rather than an enabling force, is what I call the Dependent Love Pattern. But the development of a Dependent Love Pattern isn't the result of the action of just one person. You can't point the finger at a mother, a father, or a child, and say, "It's that person's fault!"

This pattern depends on many players within the family, going beyond the mother and child, who are typically the most visible participants. Only in observing *all* the players can the complete family scene be understood—and eventually changed.

To see how this Dependent Love Pattern may emerge in actual, real-life situations, let's look briefly at the experiences of some people who have sought my help.

*John, a thirty-two-year-old businessman:* "My mother and I are very close, and we talk often about almost everything. She always wants to know how I'm doing at work and in my social activities. She wants *all* the details! And when she hears what I have to say, she always has plenty of advice ready for me, just to be sure I don't make any mistakes!

"I couldn't bear to hurt her after all she's done for me over the years, but I must say that sometimes she does get on my nerves. The other day, she unloaded on me with a lot of advice about the friends I should and shouldn't have at work and off the job. I felt like saying, 'Can't you bug off! I'm thirty-two, and I can make my own decisions!' But I didn't.

"Why does she still treat me like a baby? Frankly, as much as I love her, sometimes I think I'd like to wring her neck!'"

*Kathy, the divorced, working mother of an eight-year-old girl:* "The teacher at school called last week and said that my daughter, Sally, is having problems. She cried a lot at the beginning of the school year, and the teacher said she behaves like a little scared rabbit. She hasn't made many friends, and she acts babyish all the time.

"I just don't understand this! I've tried to give her a lot of attention since my divorce because I feel very bad about all the hurt that she's gone through. Actually, we've grown very close since the divorce, with just the two of us together in the evenings.

"My mother keeps Sally in the afternoons until I get home from work. Mom's a big help, but I do think she spoils her. She cooks whatever Sally wants to eat, and she never bothers to encourage Sally to do her homework or practice her music.

"Of course, when Mom sees that Sally is getting too far out of line, she'll try to set her straight with some nagging—just like she did with me. But still, I know Mom's an old softie at heart.

"When I finally get home in the evening, I often feel bad that I haven't had more time with Sally during the day. So I try to make up for it by doing everything I can for her before she goes to bed at night.''

*Sarah, a middle-aged homemaker:* ''Although I'm forty-five and the mother of two teenaged children, I think my mother still sees me as a child. She calls me almost every day, and she even slips over to the house and cooks dinner for us many times when she finds that I'm out in the afternoons. She's always ready with plenty of instructions on how I should deal with my children.

''I really don't understand why she's always on my case about the kids. I pick up after them, cater to them, and in general take care of them every bit as well as she took care of me. In fact, sometimes I wonder if maybe I do too much for them! I've given my life for them, but I don't think they're very grateful. In general, they seem to take me for granted and complain if I don't give them the high level of service they've come to expect.

''My oldest, Joe, graduated from high school a year and a half ago but decided not to attend college. He's been trying to find a job that appeals to him. If he could find something regular, that would at least get him out of the house and take some of the pressure off me. But every time he gets a job, he manages to lose it in a matter of weeks or months. I do love my family so much, but I'm tired and frustrated. Sometimes, I wish I could just leave the country and run away from them!''

*Sam, an adult son living at home:* ''My mother and I don't talk much, except about our problems and complaints. We end up fighting about the smallest things, often to the point of screaming at each other.

''Sometimes, I think of moving out, but then I think how hard it would be. I mean, my mother's always waited on me hand and foot. I don't even know how to cook breakfast for myself. Sure, she complains about it, and that makes me feel guilty and irresponsible. And after all, I'm not sure how well she'd do living alone. After

Dad left so many years ago, Mom sort of depended on me. Now, she always wants my advice, even if she doesn't take it. I'm not sure that either of us could get along very well if we split.''

In each of these cases, there is a strong and devoted love between mother and child. But that love, rather than being enabling, has become disabling. The distortion of love happens when a parent holds too tightly to a child, often due to the parent's own needs. Or parents may continue doing things for a child who has long left infancy behind, rather than teaching the child to do for himself. Or parents may love a great deal, but they may fail to balance that love with the encouragement of responsible independence.

## What Is the Dependent Love Pattern?

Usually, there are specific family interactions that foster such difficulties in maturing—interactions that involve the Dependent Love Pattern. In my experience of counseling people about their emotional problems, I've found that in most cases, this pattern includes four ingredients:

- *a mother who is overinvolved*—who over the years has done too much for a child and who has become overly attached to the youngster;
- *a father who is underinvolved*—who is emotionally or physically distant from the child;
- *children who don't grow up*—who remain overly dependent even as adults on their parents; and
- *grandparents who feed into the cycle*—who as parents were either overinvolved with their child, or were harsh or neglectful.

The fourth element in the pattern reflects the ongoing, multigenerational character of this family phenomenon: the smothering mother may repeat the same, overly at-

## The Dependent Love Pattern

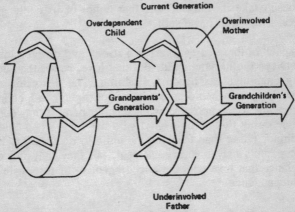

Current Generation

Overdependent Child

Overinvolved Mother

Grandparents' Generation

Grandchildren's Generation

Underinvolved Father

tentive behavior she experienced from her own mother. Or she may overreact with too much care in an effort to compensate for her more neglectful, distant parents.

## Are You an Overdependent Child?

What are some of the indications that you may have been a son or daughter in this sort of family? Test yourself against these typical traits:

- Although you're successful in some areas of your life, you still feel as though you haven't been able to move forward in other areas on your own.
- You're in a great job, but you have difficulty developing intimate peer relationships.
- You say you'd like to move out of your parents' home, but somehow, something always seems to keep you from leaving.
- You secretly worry about what Mom would do if she didn't have you to fuss over.
- You're concerned about what would happen to your

parents if you weren't around and they had to rely only on each other, without your being available to them.

- Although you're married, you still feel as though you're closer to Mom than to your husband or wife. In many ways, you feel you really haven't left home.
- It's a relief to be able to call your parents most days, or to go to their home when your spouse makes you angry.
- You sense that you don't have a genuine marriage because Mom or Dad remains a constant presence, even when you and your spouse are alone.
- Your mother-in-law, or your mother, is more in charge of your home than you are.
- Your parents' ways of doing things dictate how you think you and your spouse should operate.
- You quarrel a lot with your spouse about your parents or in-laws.
- You often feel your parents are trying to tell you how to raise your child.
- Most people think you're quite successful and you've got your life under control. But actually, you're struggling with a secret problem, such as overeating or a sexual difficulty.

These characteristics and feelings are often signals of a larger Dependent Love Pattern in a family. The child is only one of the players in this scenario. Just as important is the role of the parent.

## Are You an Overinvolved Parent?

Attentive and loving parents can sometimes be overinvolved with their children. If you are a mother, see if you recognize yourself in these descriptions of overdoing:

- You insist that your preschooler eat everything on her plate.
- You keep your child from many activities because of a desire to prevent even the slightest physical injury.
- You dress your elementary school-age child, bathe him, brush his teeth, tie his shoelaces, or otherwise act as his "valet."
- You constantly remind your ten-year-old to wear a coat on a cold day.
- You ask your fifteen-year-old if he has enough money every time he prepares to take a bus.

Some overinvolved parents engage in more extreme behavior. In my counseling practice, I've encountered parents who:

- get up four or five times a night to check on their preschooler's blanket situation;
- let their child sleep with them regularly, rather than in a bed of his own;
- infrequently allow a preschool or elementary school child to be away from their presence for very long;
- rarely allow their child to be taken care of by other people, with the result that the parents are unable to pursue their own relationship and interests and the child doesn't learn to cope with authorities other than Mom or Dad;
- sit with their nine-year-old every night until he falls asleep;
- give their child no household responsibilities;
- walk their twelve-year-old to school every day;
- constantly remind their teenager about his appointments;
- regularly do homework for or with their child;
- don't allow their teen to go out with friends, except those chosen by the parents; or
- always pick up after their teenager, who never bothers to clean up his room or belongings.

Many of these signs of excessive caring for children are most characteristic of the mother, mainly because she is traditionally the one who has been expected to be more responsible for the children. But given the family backgrounds of certain men and the shifting responsibilities in many households, some fathers may take over part or all of the smothering role in the family. Usually, however, a different role is played by the father.

## Are You an Underinvolved Parent?

When I see a mother giving excessively to the children, I often encounter certain other distinctive traits in the father of the family. If you're a father, see how many of these features of the Dependent Love Pattern describe your behavior:

- You care about your children and worry a lot about them, but you have a hard time expressing those feelings.
- You buy things for your child to show affection, rather than just saying, "I love you."
- You feel your wife nags the children or overprotects them.
- You feel your wife nags you, and you'd like to get away.
- You believe your children should have more responsibility, but because your wife is the primary caretaker, you think your views don't carry much weight.
- You get fed up with or upset by things at home. As a result, you feel a need to drink, take drugs, or look for other outlets to relax or escape.

As you can see, many of these traits of overinvolved mothers and underinvolved fathers may be found in parents of young children who haven't yet grown old enough to leave home. But the signs of the Dependent Love Pattern are not limited just to parents of small children.

I work with many parents of grown children who have become entangled in excessive dependencies. Some of these parents will allow their adult son—in his twenties, thirties, or even older—to continue to live at home, with his mother cooking, cleaning, and otherwise caring for him as she did when he was a boy. Other parents will keep in constant touch, by phone or visits, with an adult child who can't seem to function unless the parent is close at hand to provide advice and guidance. Still other overattentive mothers or fathers make decisions for a married child. In these and similar cases, the parents often feel that they are still having to do too much or are overburdened with parental duties, even though the adult child is living away from home.

In general, these are a few of the signals that tell me that I may have encountered a mother, father, or child who has become enmeshed in a Dependent Love Pattern. But is it really possible for a parent to love a child too much? Isn't receiving unconditional, all-encompassing love the key to becoming a well-adjusted person?

## Can You Love a Child Too Much?

The best way for me to answer this question is to back up and talk in more basic terms about what it takes for a child to develop into a well-adjusted, emotionally balanced adult. There are two elements children need to ensure their later emotional health: (1) a sense of personal security and belonging, and (2) a sense of competence. These are graphically described in the old saying that the two best gifts parents can give their children are roots and wings. Roots are developed by giving a youngster the assurance of continuing stable support and caring. Wings are developed by teaching, encouraging, and letting go. They enable the child to make his way in the world, to take positive action, and to realize his highest potential.

To help develop the first quality, parents must learn to show genuine love to their children. So yes, unconditional and accepting love is vital to provide children with the all-important sense of personal worth.

How well rooted is your family? Are your children getting the solid foundation of love and nurture they need? To get an idea about where you stand, try this Roots Check.

## Roots Check

If any of the following statements apply to you, put a check next to it.

\_\_\_ 1. I regularly show my child love in a physical way that's appropriate to his or her age (e.g., holding and hugging an infant; wrestling or back-patting a young child; hugging or placing an arm around children of all ages).

\_\_\_ 2. I make eye contact with my child regularly when talking with him or her.

\_\_\_ 3. I talk with and listen to each child living at home for at least ten minutes a day.

\_\_\_ 4. I compliment my child regularly on his or her strengths.

\_\_\_ 5. I tell my child I love him or her regularly.

\_\_\_ 6. Basically, I think my child is very special.

\_\_\_ 7. Overall, I see more positive than negative qualities in my child.

\_\_\_ 8. Our family has regular mealtimes and bedtimes.

\_\_\_ 9. We do fun activities together as a family.

\_\_\_ 10. I enjoy being with my child.

\_\_\_ 11. I regularly ask my child how she is doing or what she is feeling.

\_\_\_ 12. My child has a regular daily schedule.

\_\_\_ 13. My child knows I love him, even if he does something I disapprove of.

\_\_\_ 14. I spend focused-attention time regularly with my child (i.e., doing things with him without other distractions).

___ 15. I find behaviors or characteristics I like in my
child and praise them often.

If you checked each blank, your family tree is tremendously well rooted. If you have any spaces unchecked,
then go back and plan a way to build roots in those areas.
If you have less than ten spaces checked, you need to
focus on root-building—or developing greater love and
cohesion in your family. Remember: It's absolutely essential to have those roots before you try to grow wings!

In fact, let me give you a word of warning at this point:
What I've written in the following pages has been in-
tended for those who have experienced love in their families, but whose personal growth has been stunted by
overconcern and overprotectiveness. In contrast, a person who mostly lacks the basic roots of love and a sense
of worth will find it hard to grow at all.

If you find yourself feeling you never really knew
whether or not you were loved or belonged—if you've
always felt very much left alone, physically or emotionally—then this book isn't for you. But if you've been
loved, yet have never felt quite competent or able to operate completely effectively in the world, then read on
and explore the possibility of growing.

## When It's Time to Grow Wings

To help children grow, mothers and fathers must teach
responsibility and let go of their children at different
stages of their development. They must gradually encourage them to leave the safety of the family, so that the
children can begin to grow with self-confidence as they
encounter the real world. Love is absolutely essential to
help a child grow roots, but it must not interfere with the
development of a sense of competence.

Many parents do love their children, but they fail to
let go of them and allow them to learn how to function
on their own. These parents have loved too much in that

their love has become distorted into a holding-onto, doing-for attachment to the child.

In such cases, parents may find themselves dealing with perpetual children, who have never learned what it means to grow fully into adulthood. Such sons and daughters who have been loved too much—or more accurately, loved inappropriately—often fail to launch a satisfying career or establish their own successful families. They remain dependent to some degree on mothers and fathers who loved them, but who were never able to release them to become what they were meant to be. Also, children from such homes may harbor conscious or subconscious hostility toward the parents who failed to let them go. It's these children and their parents who are the main focus of this book.

Let me offer one word of caution at the outset. When you encounter an emotional problem in yourself or a loved one, try to resist the temptation to lay the blame on any particular individual. It's natural to try to single out one person as responsible for a particular set of psychological symptoms. For example, you may want to identify one youngster as a problem child, or one parent as an overprotective mother or uninvolved father.

But blaming others usually doesn't help at all. In fact, blame often increases hostility and defensiveness. When you blame, you usually ignore your responsibility and try to place it all on others. Yet who is the one person in the world whose behavior you can change? Isn't it yourself?

Usually you can begin to make helpful changes only after you understand the pattern of your entire family's interactions, including your part in the relationships. That means understanding the roles of all the family players, not just the activities and behavior of one person.

More often than not, the Dependent Love Pattern arises from a complex set of factors and circumstances involving your whole family, and even including past generations. You'll recall how many family players there tend to be, just from the simple summary of the pattern at the beginning of this chapter: (1) a mother who overwhelms the children, and sometimes the spouse, with too much involvement: (2) a father who is often distant or absent; (3) children who have remained dependent and who lack self-confidence; and (4) grandparents who are either too attentive or too neglectful. It's essential to think in terms of the family *system* that produces the pattern and not attempt to assign fault or responsibility to one individual.

Once you adopt this perspective, you'll find that there's a great deal that you, as an individual, can do to overcome the emotional difficulties stemming from this pattern in your family. If you are a parent, you can take steps to provide for your affected children. If you are a dependent child, you can learn to grow on your own. You can change your actions and reactions in relationships at home, and thereby enable other family members, as well as yourself, to begin to escape this unproductive pattern.

# Chapter 2

# THE FAMILY FACTOR

Emotional problems rarely arise in a vacuum. Instead, they tend to emerge from relationships, especially family relationships.

This family factor in emotional difficulties is fundamental to an understanding of why some parents love too much—in the sense that they overwhelm or smother their offspring with excessive involvement. It's necessary to take a close look at family interactions whenever individual problems have developed. Once we understand the family situation, we can take more effective steps to help the individual.

The family factor in emotional development includes several basic principles that underlie much of what I'll be saying throughout this book.

*Principle #1: No person is an island—and individualism has its limits.* In the United States, we have often praised "rugged individualism" and extolled individual achievement. We've been taught to think of ourselves first and to achieve at all costs, regardless of the impact on others.

17

Some popular mottoes of our day are: "Look out for number one"; "If it feels good, do it"; and "Do your own thing."

Individualism, with its impulse toward self-reliance and personal initiative, can certainly be a powerful force for positive achievement. But there are also extreme dangers that may be associated with this approach to life.

The great nineteenth-century observer of American democracy, Alexis de Tocqueville, warned about some of the possible drawbacks of individualism. As social conditions become more equal, he said, "the number of persons increases who . . . owe nothing to any man, they expect nothing from any man; they acquire the habit of always considering themselves as standing alone and they are apt to imagine that their whole destiny is in their own hands."*

In *Habits of the Heart*, by Robert Bellah and his collaborators,** we read recent case studies of American life that show how this individualism has penetrated our society and "grown cancerous" and may be doing even more serious damage than Tocqueville anticipated.

Individualism, if not properly balanced, can undercut a sense of community responsibility. The final result, in both our social and personal lives, can be the opposite of what we intend: a lack of personal achievement, group ineffectiveness, and even chaos. Yet despite these pitfalls, an individualistic approach to life has permeated much of our modern culture—including our views of psychology.

Because psychology has been deeply influenced by this individualism, much psychological thinking has focused on understanding the individual by probing internal intellectual, emotional, and biological processes. Many

*Alexis de Tocqueville, *Democracy in America*, vol. 2 (New York: Vintage Books, 1961), 105.
**Robert N. Bellah et al., *Habits of the Heart* (New York: Harper & Row, 1985).

psychotherapists seek to help individuals find personal success and happiness by encouraging them to analyze primarily their own thoughts and feelings rather than their relationship patterns. Even therapists who view parental relationships as the basis for emotional disturbances often treat individuals alone, never suggesting that those parents be included in the therapy process. They hope for progress through establishing a healing long-term therapist–patient relationship, rather than through working directly to change the ongoing relationships with parents and other significant people.

In their research and clinical observations within the last twenty-five years, however, many social scientists have linked individual emotional problems with interactional patterns within family relationships. From this has come a new understanding of people as relational beings who are a part of many larger systems of interaction. This systemic understanding has given birth to family therapy, which emphasizes how individual emotions, personalities, and problems develop—and can be changed—within the broader context of family relationships.

Salvador Minuchin, a pioneer in structural family therapy, explains, ''The old idea of the individual acting upon his environment has here become the concept of the individual interacting with his environment.'' Family therapists, he continues, understand that ''an individual's psychic life is not entirely an internal process. The individual influences his context and is influenced by it in constantly recurring sequences of interaction. . . . [and] change in a family structure contributes to changes in behavior and the inner psychic processes of the members of that system.''*

The family therapist is not interested in finding out who has been responsible for causing another person's

*Salvador Minuchin, *Families and Family Therapy* (Cambridge, Mass.: Harvard University Press, 1971), 5, 9.

emotional downfall. The idea is not to attribute blame to a mother or father. Instead, the family therapist seeks to understand important patterns of interaction among all family members over a number of generations. Then, he or she offers ways to modify those interactions to eliminate the problems.

In many ways, this kind of therapy is well suited for a self-help approach to dealing with emotional problems and difficult relationships. The family therapist mainly acts as a coach, facilitator, or consultant in helping an individual or family. The therapist expects active involvement by the client. So if you, as a layperson, can learn to observe your own interactions with others with the help of this book, you can plan strategies and work for change yourself.

As we'll see, though, effective practical action on your part begins with an understanding of your own family's interactions and relationships. You'll miss the solution if you just focus on a particular symptom or if you try to attach blame to one family member.

*Principle #2: Individual problems are often symptoms of broader family difficulties.* One young professional man, Al, was on a fast track toward upper management in his company, but he came to me because he had a writing block. Al could successfully perform the other tasks required in his job, but he couldn't seem to meet deadlines for important reports, correspondence, and other written materials. In fact, he sometimes found that he couldn't write at all when he was under pressure.

"I don't really understand what my problem is," Al said at our first meeting. "Maybe I didn't learn to write properly while I was in school. Or maybe I lack a basic talent for writing. But I thought maybe you might see some kind of special psychological defect in my personality."

In fact, the problem was not just with Al as an isolated individual. His difficulty was part of a complex set of family relationships. Although we began by discussing

Al's special struggles with writing, the discussion soon turned to his family background and his current relationship with his parents. Before long, he revealed that he still kept in close, almost daily touch with his mother.

Finally, Al admitted that unless he had Mom's help, he developed serious doubts about his ability to succeed in his job or in anything else he attempted. He felt he needed his mother's assistance to do anything worthwhile in his life. As a matter of fact, when he got into activities or responsibilities where she couldn't assist or advise him, he almost never succeeded. As you might guess, writing at work was one of those activities where Mom couldn't help him at all.

When this hard-charging young businessman understood better how his problem on the job had emerged, he began to establish a healthier, more mature relationship with his mother. Instead of continuing to relate to her fundamentally as a little child, Al started behaving more like an adult. When he disagreed with her advice, he began telling her so. While he maintained a regular, loving relationship with her, he quit asking for her thoughts on every minor detail of his life.

In addition, he began to focus on building a better relationship with his father, who had always been a background figure in family interaction. Gradually, as these relationships changed, the writing block disappeared.

Clearly, this young man's writing block wasn't an isolated, individual problem at all. It was a symptom of a larger, unbalanced family pattern. The excessively involved mother, as well as the relatively distant father, were part of broader family interactions that had been keeping the son from reaching his full professional potential. Before you can even get to first base in dealing with many emotional problems—including those arising from the Dependent Love Pattern—it's essential to recognize that those problems tend to arise from the dynamics of family life, rather than from the actions or quirks of one individual.

\* \* \*

*Principle #3: Children are part of a family, not just the product of a mother.* Too often, we've viewed children simply as products of their mothering when in reality, the mother is just one player in the larger family picture. Our society has caused us to believe the myth that Mom is somehow the person who is primarily responsible for how children turn out. The myth gains even more strength because many mothers—and especially devoted ones—are more than willing to accept the blame for their children's foibles and failures.

In fact, a woman can become a mother only if there is a father. That partnership is the basis for the family, which then teaches the child much of what he or she comes to understand about feelings and relationships. A child's sense of security and ability to deal with the struggles of life often reflect the strengths and difficulties in the marital—and parental—relationship.

Unfortunately, we may think that good mothering is sufficient for a child's development. Consequently, we may fail to realize the critical importance of both father and mother, as well as the key role of the various inter-relationships within the whole family. To understand any child, or to understand yourself, you need to put a wide-angle lens on your viewing and consider the whole family picture, of which one child is only a part.

*Principle #4: Past family patterns tend to be repeated in current relationships.* Family therapists find that patterns of past human interaction are usually repeated in some way in current relationships. For example, I often find that women who smother their children, by doing too much for them, come from families where their mothers smothered them with attention. Or sometimes, the woman's mother was neglectful or underinvolved, and this neglect has caused the woman to bounce to the opposite extreme of overinvolvement with her own children.

Unlike Freudians and other individualistic counselors,

family therapists avoid focusing heavily on past memories, or setting up situations in which you transfer your feelings about your parents to someone else, like a therapist. Instead, the family approach focuses on dealing with what's happening in your life and your relationships *today*.

Although past relationships are important, family therapists address them primarily through patterns as they are repeated in present relationships. A woman who feels her father never really loved her may find herself desperate for male attention. Or a man who feels his mother has been too involved with him may find himself avoiding intimacy with women. These issues, past and present, can be addressed by changing current relationships with parents and peers.

This emphasis on the present rather than the past should make it easier for you, the lay reader, to help yourself emotionally and to improve your family relationships. It's usually easier to change present relationships than to try to undo past hurts. By understanding and developing practical changes in the present interactions between family members, you can help undo the negative effects of both past and present.

*Principle #5: All families have rules.* Every family unit develops certain set ways of acting, with unspoken rules about how those interactions are supposed to take place.

For example, one rule in my home when I was growing up was "peace at any price." Instead of arguing about things or getting involved in any sort of conflict, we assumed it was better just to give in. Unfortunately, we also learned not to have strong opinions about different topics. This attitude could be a disadvantage for those of us who saw the need for more forceful personalities later in life. I, for one, had to unlearn some of my excessive peaceableness and work at becoming more assertive.

On the other hand, there were certain strengths in our family pattern. For one thing, we learned to be great accommodators and facilitators—qualities that can be quite helpful for those in fields like therapy or business negotiation.

A family I once worked with had the opposite rule. They assumed that you must never be wrong. In that group, the members constantly put each other down; they always criticized and never apologized. If they admitted they were wrong about anything, they automatically became failures! Such a background may encourage the development of strong personalities—a result that may be quite good. But family members may also become unsympathetic and inflexible. As a result, they may be difficult to work with in team situations requiring group cooperation outside the family.

Other family rules I've run into include:

- Don't contradict Grandmother.
- Don't upset Dad.
- If you want Dad to know something, tell Mom.
- Go to Mom first if you want a "yes" answer.
- Don't leave Mom alone.
- Leave it on the floor—Mom will take care of it.
- Children are to be seen and not heard.
- Children come first . . . or last.

How about your own family? What rules prevailed, and perhaps still prevail, in your home?

One way to check on this is to keep your eyes and ears open the next time you visit your parents. Even though you may be functioning as a perfectly capable adult away from home, when you reenter your family circle, you will most likely be sucked into the family atmosphere. Along with your parents and brothers and sisters, you'll begin to act and react as you did when you were much younger. In other words, you'll operate according to the family rules.

These five basic principles underlie much of what we'll be saying as we explore the phenomenon of love–hate relationships in your family. Once you have become attuned to the family factor in your life, you'll need to take a closer look at your own family and try to recognize its own special patterns. In other words, you'll have to determine your family type.

# Chapter 3

# WHAT'S YOUR FAMILY TYPE?

When people think in terms of individuals, they often think of personality types, such as the "outgoing person," the "introvert," or the "nurturing personality." Similarly, when you recognize you're part of a bigger family system, it's helpful to begin to understand yourself and your relationships in terms of family types.

Even if you are miles away from your parents or if they have been dead for years, you have learned your basic patterns of interacting, or not interacting, in close family relationships. You bring these same patterns and feelings into your current relationships.

To understand yourself better, think for a moment about your own family. Try to answer these questions:

- Who's in it? Think both of your nuclear and extended families.
- How close or distant are various members to each other?
- How clear are the roles in the family?
- How are differences handled?

- What are your family rules?
- How flexible or rigid are these rules?

Now that you've answered these questions, let's consider the characteristics of four basic family types to see if you can place your own family in a category. Remember as you do this that even though every family is unique, most do tend toward one type or another. Each of the four types will be described in their extremes, to help you more easily recognize their characteristic features with their strengths and weaknesses.*

The purpose of thinking in types is not to pigeonhole your family, but to help you recognize your family's characteristics. Identifying your family type is your first step toward learning to make the best use of your family's strengths and to overcome your family's weaknesses.

*Type #1: The Free-Wheeling Family.* Generally speaking, this family is characterized by little structure or order. There may be a lack of scheduling for meals or bedtimes. Different family members tend to do what they want to do, with little overall planning and few joint family activities.

On the whole, there are few rules in this family about what constitutes right or wrong conduct. Those rules that do exist may be contradictory. For example, a child may be allowed to watch television before he does his homework on some days. But on other days, he may be told TV before homework is unacceptable. Finally, this family tends to be crisis-prone. There always seems to be a major problem with the children at school, the parents at work, or some upsetting circumstance in social engagements.

Certainly, despite such a high level of activity or even

---

*For an expanded discussion of family types, see Gerda L. Schulman, *Family Therapy: Teaching, Learning, Doing* (Washington, D.C.: University Press of America, 1982).

chaos, there can be advantages to growing up in a family of this type. For one thing, individual members tend to develop a high level of independence. This family is typically flexible and adaptable when there's a need to change or to respond in different ways to different situations. An unexpected visitor isn't likely to create many problems for parents or children who are already accustomed to constant disruptions and surprises.

But the free-wheeling family has weaknesses as well as strengths. The lack of structure and order tends to leave family members without a sufficient sense of stability and security. As a result, they may live in a constant state of confusion, as they move from one crisis to the next. Parents in this type of family group tend not to become deeply involved in their parenting role or in setting limits. Children are left without as much early parental nurturing, leadership, or home teaching as they may need.

*Type #2: The Disciplined Family.* This family has relatively rigid rules that allow little flexibility for individual members. There tends to be a clear hierarchy, with parents at the top and children at the bottom. Consequently, the disciplined family may have little warmth in parent–child relations.

Despite some rigidity, the disciplined family can provide a certain security for children because parental roles and the boundaries of acceptable behavior are clearly delineated. There's also usually some orderliness and certainty in the human relationships, which keeps crises and chaos at a minimum.

On the other hand, this type of family group has weaknesses. The rigidity and lack of warmth of the ''top parent'' can create fear in the children, and in the subordinate spouse as well. One danger in a family where discipline is supreme is the possibility of child and spouse abuse.

The rigid structure of the relationships and the excessive number of rules under which members have to operate may also foster a dependency in the children. This influence may seriously undercut the development of independence and creativity during adulthood.

Furthermore, the lack of independence may make it very difficult for children to leave home gracefully. They may find that they're constantly under the thumb of their parents and can't leave at all. In contrast, they may make a dramatic break away from the family circle, for example, by running away or becoming pregnant.

*Type #3: The "Down" Family.* In this family group, there's often limited communication between members, and energy levels tend to be relatively low. There's a pervasive sadness in this family. Typically, there's no joking or camaraderie. Members either tend to drift off by themselves, or they become fragmented into isolated subgroups. On the whole, those who are trapped in a depressed, isolated family have a great deal of trouble moving out to form relationships with individuals or groups on the outside.

Although there are many problems with this type of family, it does have at least one strength: members have usually had to cope with so many problems or losses that they have developed expertise in their coping skills. Consequently, they may be able to handle death, divorce, or other tragedies with fewer emotional repercussions than those from other family systems.

On the other hand, the weaknesses in this type of family are significant. The isolation can lead to all sorts of individual emotional problems, such as chronic depression and underachievement. The general malaise or lack of energy makes it difficult for individual members, or for the family as a whole, to provide for basic needs. In some circumstances, this family may even find it hard to survive. For example, unemployment may become a common problem for the breadwinners. The lack of interaction among family members may produce an emo-

tional shallowness and weakness in the individuals. As a
result, both children and parents become unable to move
forward or establish productive relationships with those
in the outside world.

*Type #4: The Devoted Family.* The primary characteristic
of this family type is close relationships that may take
priority over independent thought or action. For example, family members may expect others to know what
they are thinking or feeling, to almost read each other's
minds; and they may constantly finish sentences for one
another. Family members usually like to be with others
rather than alone: Mom or Dad or Brother or Sister may
have to be present for an individual to feel most comfortable.

In addition, roles may be flexible in the devoted family. Although the family consists of a variety of people
of various ages, everyone in the family may tend to be
treated in the same way, with the differences in their roles
not precisely detailed or defined. At times, for instance,
the mother may do everything for the child and expect
unthinking obedience, while at other times, the mother
may actually be depending on the child to care for her.

With such role confusion, it's not surprising that the
devoted family may have weak boundaries between parents and children. In some families of this type, the parents may enjoy very little privacy because they have failed
to set sufficient limits on their interactions with their children. The father and mother may find that they can't enjoy themselves in bed together or even be alone in the
bathroom without having a child barge in on them.

There are many strengths in this type of family unit,
including a tremendous amount of care and support
among the various members. A sense of closeness as
well as a special esprit and loyalty bind the family unit
together.

On the other hand, there are also a number of weaknesses in the devoted family. The overly close and in-

volved relationships among members may leave little room for personal identity, the development of individuality, or the exercise of responsibility. The lack of clear boundaries between parents and children, and the lack of delineation of roles in the family, may cause the daily functioning of the household to become unnecessarily complex and confused.

Finally, the children from this family may have difficulty in developing friendships, exercising responsibility, or otherwise becoming independent outside the family circle.

In this book, we'll be concerned primarily with problems related to the Devoted Family type. Of course, just as no one person fits exactly into any personality type, so too no family fits exactly into one of these four structural types. Each family is unique in the way its particular members function and relate to one another. Still, thinking in term of these four categories can be quite useful in understanding your family and working to build on strengths while improving on weaknesses.

Did you recognize your own family type from these descriptions? Your family may fit perfectly into one of the categories. Then again, it may have some characteristics from several family types, though it probably resembles one more than the others.

Remember, though, that classifying your family within a family type says very little about its relative health or problems. Families within each type may be relatively strong, or relatively weak. So for example, one Devoted Family may be quite warm and close, and may have found ways to allow for individual differences. Another Devoted Family may be extremely close and caring, but not able to encourage its members to move out on their own. The ultimate goal is not to change your family type, but to build on the strengths and mitigate the weaknesses.

To the degree that your family has characteristics of the Devoted Family, whether they are many or few, then this book is written for you. The Dependent Love Pattern we'll be exploring arises directly out of the relationships characteristic of the Devoted Family.

If your family has only some of the characteristics of the Devoted Family, you might use this book to try to grow more loving and nurturing. At the same time, you should be able to learn some ways to teach responsibility and encourage independence in your children.

Whatever your family situation, you must beware of pointing the finger of blame at others. For example, if your family has many characteristics of the Free-Wheeling Family, you should be especially cautious about any judgmental use of this book. You may find yourself identifying others as coming from Devoted Families and then smugly congratulating yourself on not being like them. Such an attitude is likely to be an indication of your own family difficulties in developing closeness, structure, and stability. Rather than pointing a finger, try to learn from devoted families by trying to adopt some of their best characteristics. Your devoted family friends—or spouse—may get ideas from you about how to be more autonomous and spontaneous. But perhaps you need to learn loyalty, commitment, and warmth from them.

Now that you have some idea of your family type—and what that tells you about how to use the book—we'll examine how some of these relationships can give rise to the Dependent Love Pattern.

# Chapter 4

# THE DEPENDENT
# LOVE PATTERN

"I'm forty years old, and I can't live my own life without constantly trying to please my father!"

"I'm thirty, married with a family, yet my mother still insists on treating me like a five-year-old!"

"I'm twenty-five, and I wonder if maybe I should think about moving out of my folks' home and starting my own life."

"I'm sixty, and I'd expected to start living a more relaxed life, without so much responsibility for my children. But it seems the older I get, the more involved I become with my kids' marriages, finances, and families."

The key to many such individual emotional problems, and to many difficulties in human relationships, is the Dependent Love Pattern. The salient feature of this dependent love is a caring concern that has become a stifling overinvolvement.

As you'll recall, there are usually four main elements in this pattern as it plays itself out in a family:

- an overly involved mother,
- an emotionally distant or absent father,
- children who are overly dependent, and
- grandparents who have been either overinvolved or neglectful toward their children.

Of course, no short description of a complex emotional or family pattern will apply in every case. Often, one or more of these four characteristics may not be present—even though the key ingredients of parental overinvolvement and child dependency may be there. For example, the father may not be emotionally distant at all. He may smother right along with the mother! Or the mother may be distant and the father may be overinvolved.

There are many such variations, and there is also a variety of reasons why they may arise. In the typical devoted family with this dependency problem, however, the above factors will often be present.

But just what does this dependent love look like in a family? How exactly do these factors emerge and interact in real-life situations? To answer these questions, let's take a look at some challenges that confronted an actual family who found themselves having to deal with the Dependent Love Pattern.

## The Story of Successful Sandra

Sandra, an attractive young woman of twenty-seven, came from a three-child family that seemed ideal, at least on the surface. Among other things, the family members appeared to be quite devoted to one another. They were regular churchgoers, with high standards of morality. In addition, there were outward signs of success among the children: At least two of the three—Sandra and her younger brother—were upwardly mobile, with good school records, good jobs, and a relatively high need to achieve.

Both her mother and father were well educated, and they had apparently succeeded in their marriage. In any case, they mentioned no significant problems in the thirty years they had been together. Furthermore, they had never wanted for material things. The father, a successful restaurateur, had always been an excellent provider, but the demands of his business required him to work long hours and be away from home a great deal. As a result, the children often saw him only on the weekends, and then he was usually too tired from the week's work to spend much time with them in their activities.

Sandra's mother did her best to make up for the father's absence. She stayed at home as a full-time homemaker and caretaker for the children, and I think she genuinely enjoyed being around the children and bringing them up. She had come from a family where she felt she had received too little love from her mother and father, and she wanted to be sure she didn't make the same mistake. So she tended to go overboard in being sure that each of her three children received her full attention.

Sandra, the eldest of the three, had always dated regularly. But even though she said she wanted to settle down and get married, she had not yet found the right man. Her brother Gary, the middle child, was two years younger than Sandra. He had been married for about three years, already had one child, and was doing rather well as a salesman for a computer firm. The youngest of the children, Ellen, was twenty-two years old and still lived at home. She had dropped out of college and worked at a number of jobs, but she hadn't lasted at any of them for very long.

Of the three, Sandra was the highest achiever. In fact, she seemed the epitome of the modern-day yuppie, or young urban professional. She had already moved into a management position in her company, and a salary in the mid-five-figure range had enabled her to buy a condominium, an expensive car, and an ample wardrobe.

But all was not perfect in Sandra's life. She came to

me because she had been wrestling with a problem of bulimia. She would behave with perfect propriety in her business and social relationships during the day. Typically, she would succeed in practically anything she attempted. But while relaxing at home after a stressful day, she might suddenly eat a whole package of cookies or two bags of potato chips. Then, she would go into the bathroom and literally throw up everything she'd just eaten.

I could see, almost immediately, that the problems Sandra was facing were not hers alone. Rather, she was part of a broader family interaction we've defined as the Dependent Love Pattern. As a result, I asked the entire family to come in to see me for a few sessions so that I could get a better idea of the full scope of their difficulties. With this information, I hoped to suggest some ways to help Sandra, as well as the other family members who were involved.

Our first family meeting was rather traumatic. Both Sandra's mother and Ellen burst into tears within the first minutes, apparently because they were so upset to be sitting in a therapist's office. Just the fact that they were sitting there seeking help was an admission that their family situation was not as perfect as they had imagined it to be.

As we proceeded with the discussion, it became evident that Sandra's family was a classic case of the Dependent Love Pattern. Specifically, the mother, reacting to a lack of love in her own family, had been overly attentive, concerned, and caring about Sandra, as well as about her other two children. The father, with his frequent absences from home because of work and his inability to express himself emotionally, was a relatively distant figure in the family. Each of the children, in his or her own ways, showed the impact of these influences in unhealthy dependencies.

First, let's consider Sandra. She had always been successful in task-oriented projects, both in her schoolwork and in extracurricular activities. Even though she was attractive and socially polished, however, she had few close, satisfying peer friendships.

But Sandra said she didn't really miss those personal ties with others her own age. The reason? Her mother had been caring and understanding about Sandra's needs, and the two got into the habit of talking together regularly, like the best of girlfriends. Sandra had grown to rely on her mother as her most trusted confidante.

As for Sandra's father, he was a gentle, dependable man who was willing to do errands and favors for her and provide her with money when she needed it. But he made very little attempt to engage in genuine personal communication with her and rarely encouraged her in her goals or activities.

On a very deep level, Sandra wanted a closer relationship with her father, but he just wasn't available. So she did what might seem to be the next best thing to establishing a real relationship. In an effort to get closer to him or win his attention in some way, she began to work hard, as he did, to get praise from him for being a star at school.

Unfortunately, though, Dad wasn't home too much because he was overseeing his restaurant business. But Sandra, still fervently wanting him to be more of a presence in her life, in effect tried to invoke his presence by eating with the same gusto at the dinner table that she knew he did. As a result, she began to put on far too much weight.

When Sandra was about twelve years old, she discovered boys and found in them a possible alternative source for the male attention she craved. So she dieted to improve her figure, and the dieting was done like her schoolwork, to obsessive perfection. She slowly began to starve herself. Before long, the school guidance counselor noticed Sandra's problem and feared that the girl might be suffering from anorexia nervosa. The counselor brought the matter to her parents' attention.

Sandra, feeling considerable adult scrutiny and pressure, still managed to find a way to satisfy the grownups *and* stay thin: She would go into the bathroom after a meal and secretly throw up. That way, she was able to achieve all her objectives. She could imitate her father's eating habits and yet at the same time keep her weight down and be in a position to attract boys her age. But of course, no one in the family was aware of the weight-control method she had chosen. She wouldn't dare upset the harmony in her home by sharing this secret.

Under the direction of her mother, Sandra decided to enter a middle-level college near her home. Although her grades would have qualified her for entrance to a top-flight school, she was intent on being a big fish in a little pond—mainly so that she could continue to be a star for her family.

As she had expected, she did quite well in this college, graduating with high honors and gaining admission to an excellent, nationally recognized business school. Then, after two more years of study, she graduated with an MBA and went on to the corporate management position that she held when I originally met her. Unfortunately, however, the bulimia persisted.

Throughout her school years and early professional life, Sandra continually encountered difficulties in her relationships with people her own age. As a young adult, she still had almost no close young women friends, and her mother continued to play the role of her best friend and main confidante. They frequently went shopping together on weekends and spent hours discussing Sandra's work life and personal aspirations.

During many of these conversations, the mother would express her own worries about life and provide plenty of advice and guidance for Sandra. Sandra, for her part, would at times agree with her mother's concerns, and at other times she would argue intensely. But she'd never simply state her differences clearly and quietly. In short, they had developed a classic love–hate, mother–daughter relationship.

Sandra's relationships with men were also fraught with problems. Over the years, her need for male attention had become so great that she *always* had to have a boyfriend and if she broke up with one boyfriend, she would have to find a new one immediately. She would never appear for a date unless she was perfectly dressed and made up, and she further felt compelled to please her boyfriends sexually in order to win their approval.

Although she had been told by her highly moral mother that she should not have sex before she got married, Sandra's intense need for male approval had caused her to reject that advice before she graduated from high school. Soon, she was involved in rather promiscuous relationships with a series of young men, and the pattern of these relationships often resembled her eating binges. She would hold off from sexual involvements as long as she could, but then she would lose control and inevitably end up in bed with whomever she was seeing. Tremendous guilt and a sense of failure would overwhelm her immediately after these encounters, and she would avoid sex for several weeks, when she found herself losing control again.

Despite her close relationship with her mother, Sandra didn't breathe a word about these sexual escapades. She sensed, quite rightly, that her mother would have been devastated to hear the facts of her daughter's private life. Despite Sandra's best efforts to discipline herself, her bulimia also persisted. Even though Sandra was a model of success externally, her internal struggles were destroying her body and her relationships with other people.

The ongoing, intergenerational nature of the Dependent Love Pattern also became clear as we discussed Sandra's grandparents. Sandra's father's family had spent a lot of time near each other in a physical sense because they had all worked together in a family business, but they had spent little time talking together or developing an understanding of personal relationships.

As I've already mentioned Sandra's mother's mother

had been rather cold, and Sandra's mother's father had often been overbearing and unreliable. As a result, Sandra's mother had felt uncared for and unloved when she was a youngster. To compensate for this lack, she wanted to make sure that she didn't fall into a similar trap with her own children. As a result, she overreacted, by doing too much for them.

Although Sandra's mother was unusually involved in Sandra's life, she wasn't one to play favorites. She was also quite attentive toward her other children—but with somewhat different results. Gary still kept in constant touch with his mother, who provided him with a steady stream of advice and concern. He and his family spent almost every holiday with his parents. On those occasions, underlying tensions usually mounted between the mother and her daughter-in-law, who felt threatened by the control Gary's mother continued to exercise over him. At one point, there even seemed some danger that Gary's marriage might be on the verge of breaking up. But the birth of his first child relieved some of the pressure because his mother now began to focus her excessive attention on her new grandchild.

The youngest child, twenty-two-year-old Ellen, showed some of the most unsettling symptoms of all. She seemed to have become immobilized by her mother's smothering tendencies, and consequently, she had never left home. In fact, even though she had been trained as a secretary, she seemed to have trouble holding down a regular job.

Typically, she would begin to work with some business but then would quickly become dissatisfied. Usually, she would either leave after a few months or do something that would get her fired. Although everyone in the family was worried about Ellen, her presence at home at least gave her mother an ongoing job of caring and worrying about someone.

Ellen, then, had become totally ineffectual because of a number of family influences that were bearing down upon her. Although her mother said she was concerned about Ellen, she also secretly worried about what she would do with herself when her youngest child left home. In turn Ellen was worried that her mother's happiness and the health of her parents' marriage still depended on her presence.

At the same time, Ellen had started to become a kind of emotional punching bag for her normally mild-mannered father. He had been feeling some frustrations at work as well as annoyance with his wife. So his youngest child's presence provided a ready target for his anger. As he saw it, she was lazy and a freeloader, sitting there at home not working and failing to make the most of her potential. He constantly put her down with subtle, cynical remarks—a practice that triggered periodic arguments and increasingly hard feelings between him and his wife.

To round out the picture, Sandra went regularly to Ellen to discuss certain sensitive matters that she didn't feel comfortable revealing to her mother. In particular, Sandra liked to unload some of her frustrations with her boyfriends during these sisterly sessions.

The younger woman felt increasingly weighed down with her family's massive emotional burdens. She had no opportunity to develop her own identity—no sense of who she was as an independent person in her own right. Consequently, she could not function competently in the outside world.

SOME SOLUTIONS FOR SANDRA AND HER LOVED ONES

During my therapy sessions with this family, a number of encouraging developments occurred. First, the family members began to discard their ''perfect family'' mask and started speaking more openly about the troubles they were experiencing. Before long, they were able to take steps to begin changing the overinvolvement of the mother and the underinvolvement of the father in the family's emotional life.

Sandra's father began to realize the important role he

## Sandra's Family's Dependent Love Pattern

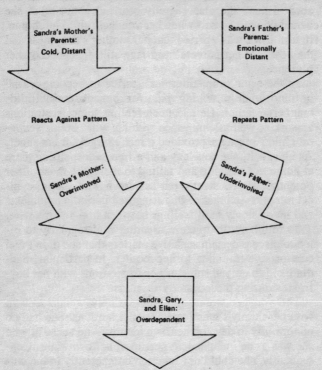

Sandra's Mother's Parents: Cold, Distant

Sandra's Father's Parents: Emotionally Distant

Reacts Against Pattern

Repeats Pattern

Sandra's Mother: Overinvolved

Sandra's Father: Underinvolved

Sandra, Gary, and Ellen: Overdependent

had in the family. He had to learn not only to be physically home more often, but also to be ready to listen and talk with his wife and children. He actually began to take his wife out on dates occasionally, and he would now initiate calls to the children.

Sandra's mother learned to ask her husband in specific ways for the emotional support she had grown accustomed to looking for from her children. She also took steps to develop new outside interests of her own.

As for the children, Sandra's mother learned to show her care by encouraging all three of them to exercise greater freedom and independence. She could now be heard to say, "I'm busy right now." Or, "I think you can handle that." Or, "Have you talked to some of your friends about that?"

As these changes were occurring in their parents, the children gave up their inappropriate dependent roles of being Mother's companion, her emotional support, or her "job" at home. They learned to take on responsibilities both inside and outside their family, rather than just relying on "good ol' Mom."

Of course, these changes didn't happen all at once. There were many delays and false starts along the way. At first, Sandra's mother became quite lonely and filled much of her time by wistfully watching the neighbors' children in their backyards for hours on end.

Gradually, though, she learned to let go of her children. She began to "take a vacation from her worries," as we put it in our discussions during therapy. Her husband came to realize his importance at home and learned to give his wife a hand to hold and a shoulder to cry on.

At the outset, Dad did have a hard time with the increased closeness. When he first took his wife to the movies as part of their new relationship, they went to separate movies in the same theater! But little by little, he came to enjoy the emotional togetherness that he had never known in his own family. Eventually, he progressed so well that his wife found him to be a much better and more mature focus for her love than the children, whom she had tried to smother with her attention.

But how about the children? How did they respond to the new patterns of behavior in their family?

Ellen had been facing a potentially dangerous emotional situation if she had continued on the passive path that she was following. But with encouragement and release from her stifling family roles, she was able to devote her natural sensitivity and energy to outside friendships and to her own school and career goals. Within a couple of months, she had moved out of her parents' home and was pursuing a much more active and healthy personal life.

Gary, the married son, didn't involve himself directly in our later therapy sessions, but he did seem to benefit from the changing family patterns. As his mother intervened less in his family, the pressures on his wife abated. As a result, Gary, his wife, and their children were able to develop their own independent identity as a family group. They even started taking their own family vacations, without feeling pressure to join members of Gary's family.

As for Sandra, she has had to lower her standards of perfection in many areas of her life—with beneficial results. Among other things, she now no longer has trouble with bulimia. She has to remain attentive to her emotional and physical health when the stresses on her begin to build up—and that means finding positive ways to release the pressures.

Sandra also has made significant progress in her relationships with men. She finally understood that a major reason for her promiscuity was her need for male affection, which she had been unable to find with her father. Because Sandra craved male attention so much, she had failed to establish and follow her own standards in sexual relationships. In many cases, the men had set the standards of behavior, and Sandra proceeded to do whatever they wanted of her.

She finally realized how her unbalanced views toward men had gotten her into trouble. Eventually, she found that regardless of what the men wanted, she was able to abide by the standards that she felt, down deep, were right. As she and her father began to talk more openly and as she developed more supportive female friendships, her desperate need for a constant male companion decreased. She even discovered she could relate to men as friends, and not just as lovers.

As you can see, Sandra's family had tried to be loving, caring, and helpful toward one another. From the beginning, all family members had been deeply concerned about the others and had expressed their care in the only way they understood. But the Dependent Love Pattern had thrown everything out of balance, distorted relationships, and produced a variety of emotional problems. By adjusting those relationships, the family members were able to relieve many of the pressures that had produced the emotional difficulties and frustrations.

Sandra's family is just one example of a much broader problem that results when a loving parent loves inappropriately. To understand better some of the dimensions of the Dependent Love Pattern, let's now explore briefly some of the typical characteristics of this pattern.

## How Devotion
## Turns Into Dependent Love

The devoted family is basically a healthy, strong family type that can provide a solid foundation of self-worth for children and a generally helpful network of supportive relationships. But when healthy, balanced love is transformed into a kind of enmeshment, characterized by excessive, overbearing parental involvement without allowing individual expression, emotional trouble may not be far behind. Loving may turn into smothering.

What does this dependent love look like in a devoted family? What are the most obvious signs that devotion has become overwhelming for a child? The first clue arises when loving devotion blurs the natural boundary between parent and child. The second clue appears when caring involvement stifles individual identity, expression, and autonomy.

*Blurred boundaries.* In every family, it's important to have roles that are clearly understood, or to know "who's who" in a relationship. The most critical boundary or distinction between roles is that between parents and children.

This parent–child boundary often becomes blurred in overly involved families. Parent–child relationships take on a more peer-like quality tending to exclude age and role differences.

For example, instead of having more appropriate friends their own age, a mother and daughter may be each other's best friend. Mom may confide in her son rather than her husband, or Dad may look to his daughter for affirmation and companionship. Brothers and sisters may be split between parents, rather than enjoying youthful fun together or joining forces occasionally against Mom and Dad. One parent and a child may become allies in influencing family decisions and consistently find themselves opposing the other parent or possibly another child.

*Stifled individualism.* In devoted families, there's a strong sense of the family as a unit, but this attitude can develop at the expense of individual identity. Closeness may become so important that there is little room for individual freedom or for the development of boundaries between individuals.

As a result, there may be little respect for the rights of the individual or little recognition of the importance of individual identity. Even clothes and toilet articles may be shared on a regular basis, as though they have become common property.

In short, a child, "Maria Rodriguez," may be most importantly a "Rodriguez," and not a "Maria." She may be stifled from developing as a teenager who has her own tastes and ambitions.

Typically, you'll see a lot of communication back and forth in this type of family. But expression of any individual difference is taboo. In the most dependent families, individuals often interrupt or finish one another's sentences. There can be an almost clairvoyant sense that you know—or ought to know—what your brother, sister, or parents are going to say or feel.

Individuals who express their own opinions or make their own decisions apart from the family as a whole can be construed as hostile and a threat to family unity. Even such small expressions of individuality as closing the bedroom door—or, heaven forbid, locking it!—may be severely frowned upon. Often, members of this kind of family group are reluctant to tell other members to "knock before entering."

Members of devoted families usually spend a lot of time together in common activities, including eating, sleeping, shopping, talking, and even fighting. Togetherness can be so important in the enmeshed devoted family that separations of any kind may be regarded as a threat. If a child wants to go to a friend's house overnight, the parents may raise all sorts of questions and eventually deny the request. Many times, the parents don't see such an overnight outing as a normal interest—though in fact, it's quite appropriate for children of elementary age and older.

When a fifteen-year-old daughter expresses an interest in a boyfriend, the mother or father may wrongly interpret that interest as an indication that the youngster somehow thinks less of her parents. Similarly, when an eighteen-year-old wants to go away to college, that perfectly normal expression of independence may be viewed as a revolt.

In one family situation, a twenty-one-year-old daughter suggested to her mother that she would like to get a job in a nearby city and set up her own apartment. The mother then accused the daughter of contemplating an act tantamount to prostitution!

Devoted families that develop a Dependent Love Pattern usually focus so much on providing nurturing and closeness that they fail in the parental task of *enabling*, or teaching individual responsibility and autonomy. They may not recognize the need to enable their child to perform, or they may expect the school to take care of this part of early development. Nearly always, the parents are fearful of losing the sense of tight oneness as a family.

## How Individuality Is Stifled

There are a number of ways that devoted families may curb individual identity and discourage a child from functioning on his own. Often, this negative influence is not intentional, but occurs in subtle, routine patterns of interaction. Let me describe a few typical practices that I've observed.

*Doing too much for others.* One characteristic of devotion is a willingness to do for others. A devoted mother is attentive to her child's every need and ready to do whatever she can to meet it. Yet ironically, if she continues to do for her child rather than teach her child to do for himself, her action, which is motivated by love, may actually cripple the object of her affection.

Let's take a simple example to illustrate. When a baby is little, a parent dresses the child out of a desire to show attentive care. If the parent continues to do this as the child grows up, however, the child will remain an emotional baby because he won't even know how to get dressed.

While few if any mothers dress a ten-year-old, many continue to do things for their child which the child could easily do for himself. These include cleaning rooms, packing lunches, and washing dishes, just to name a few. Believe it or not, when a parent continues to do for a child those things that the child could do for himself, the youngster may feel the parent doesn't think he's capable of doing the task himself. Instead of experiencing love, the child may actually feel put down.

*Serving rather than teaching.* Parents often understand clearly their responsibility to feed, clothe, and clean, but they fail to see the parental responsibility to teach their children gradually how to do those same things for themselves.

Parents in devoted families too often assume the role of servant rather than teacher. A mother might fix five different special foods or meals for a child in one day. Yet she may not take fifteen minutes to instruct the child about how to prepare her own food. These parents' great involvement with their children simply doesn't include a serious effort at teaching or training the children to become independent. Yet the goal of all good parenting should be to raise a mature adult child who is able to care for himself.

Typically, parents who have become part of a Dependent Love Pattern will take over for or criticize their children when the youngsters are attempting to do something new, but still aren't able to perform it too well. The mother or father may say in a seemingly nice voice, "Here, honey, let me do that for you," or, "You just can't do it right." Consequently, the child never learns the skills.

*Speaking for others.* Devoted family members often speak for each other, rather than allow each person to speak for himself. This occurs as frequent interruptions as one person will finish another's sentence. Or perhaps one person will agree or disagree with another before anyone has even completed a thought.

In another typical situation, someone might ask a daughter what her favorite food is, and her mother might give the answer. Or if the daughter speaks briefly, the mother may explain or elaborate further.

Children in these situations may feel confused when they are not really allowed to speak for themselves, but instead are expected to speak with the others in a larger "family voice." When children are not encouraged to feel, think, and talk for themselves, they gradually become emotionally mute or terribly angry.

* * *

*Holding on for a parent's sake.* When children are very young, they need to be held and watched closely. Although this need to be held is critical for every child, the close holding or constant presence of a parent can also fulfill many needs in the parent—especially in the parent who didn't receive much holding herself as a youngster.

As the child grows, he will naturally need and desire to move on from a tight closeness with his parents to more independence. But the parent who has a great emotional hunger that's satisfied by holding a child may continue to hold on more intensely and for a longer time than is necessary. Unfortunately, this well-meant loving hold, which may somehow be fulfilling for the parent, may become an emotional choke-hold for the child.*

You are beginning to understand how healthy, caring love may subtly turn into a stifling dependent love. At the same time, however, perhaps you're wondering how balanced your own family is in its loving. To check this, take the following quiz and see how many of the dependent love traits apply to you and your family.

### Are You Part of a
### Dependent Love Pattern?

Consider these characteristic attitudes and situations, which can be found in many devoted families. How many of them do you recognize in your own family, and to what degree are they present?

\_\_ 1. Most doors to rooms are left open. People rarely close a door for privacy, except to change clothes.

\_\_ 2. Family members try to sense how the others are feeling, without words necessarily being ex-

*"Hunger Versus Love: A Perspective on Parent-Child Relations" video in association with Dr. Robert Firestone. A presentation of The Glendon Association, Los Angeles, Calif.

changed. Some family members rely on this intuition or "mind reading" quite heavily.

___ 3. Often, one person will finish another's sentence. Or, a person will leave a sentence unfinished, assuming that the others know how it's supposed to end.

___ 4. Most family members always want to be accompanied by another family member when they go to the store, for a walk, or on some other outing.

___ 5. Children of different ages tend to be treated much the same way, with similar bedtimes, allowances, and rules for outside friendships.

___ 6. The parents and children in the household don't have well-established, separate roles.

___ 7. Parents have little time or space that is designated for them alone.

___ 8. One parent may often side with a child against the other parent.

___ 9. The children rarely do things together as just a group of kids, without a parent along.

___ 10. Family togetherness is an extremely important "family rule," especially at holidays, and any exceptions to the rule cause tremendous distress.

___ 11. People outside the family circle are not regarded as part of the "real" family, even if they are welcomed into the home as visitors.

___ 12. A child's leaving home is a huge and difficult event for the family.

___ 13. In the parents' eyes, boyfriends or girlfriends tend not to be good enough for the family member they're dating.

___ 14. A grandparent in the house may still treat the adult parent as a child, or the grandparent may consistently side with a grandchild against the parent.

___ 15. Several people may be responsible for the same duties or chores in the household. Consequently, there's no clarity of roles.

___ 16. Belongings such as clothes or toys may often be shared in the family, without any clear sense of personal possession.

___ 17. Parents make frequent calls to adult children who are living outside the home.

___ 18. Parents have a key to their adult child's home, and tend to walk in and out without necessarily calling ahead of time or knocking.

___ 19. Mother does most of the cooking or cleaning, even for teenagers or adult children who are living at home. She tends to perform these household tasks with little or no help from adult children when they come home for a visit.

___ 20. The mother constantly reminds children of elementary school age and older to wear appropriate clothing for the weather.

___ 21. The mother worries a lot about the children's diets and may cook separate things at separate times to try to ensure good, nutritious eating. Mom may complain often about the children's unusual eating habits.

___ 22. Children past preschool age have difficulty going to sleep on their own in their own bed. They may also have trouble staying in their own bed throughout the night.

___ 23. The mother selects the clothes for the children and engages in debates with them about the appropriate style of dress, even when they're well past preschool age.

___ 24. Parents may feel left out or hurt when a child wants to visit friends.

___ 25. The father allows the grown child to join him in his business but requires easier or lower work standards than he does of the other employees.

___ 26. The father does not want his teenage daughter to be out without supervision or to be required to do many chores around the home until she's married.

___27. Although parents may complain of children being lazy or not doing their part around the home, in the end they tend to do the children's work for them.

___28. Parents spend much time nagging, helping, or otherwise being involved in the child's homework.

___29. If the child forgets something he's responsible for—such as his lunch, books, or bus money—the parent will usually take it to the child, rather than having the youngster bear the natural consequences.

___30. Parents think they give "everything" to their children, but they often feel that the youngsters are not grateful.

___31. When the children are out doing something on their own, the parents worry so much that they often have difficulty proceeding with their own personal activities.

___32. It's hard for a child to decide to get married. The commitment may occur only after an agonizing, extended courtship. Or to avoid the agony of the decision, the child may just act on impulse and get married on the spur of the moment.

___33. No matter how much the children try to do for their parents, or the parents for the children, the one who is giving always seems to feel that he hasn't done quite enough.

Certainly, not every devoted family will have all of these characteristics. But if you find that even five of these traits apply to your family, then your family is probably the devoted family type, and you may easily be caught up in a Dependent Love Pattern. If you can recognize this tendency early and make appropriate adjustments, you may be able to avoid serious problems later.

Even if you have more serious, deeply ingrained problems in your family relationships, there's still plenty of hope for correcting the situation. As we've already seen, family members with significant emotional problems have been able to break free of the Dependent Love Pattern by taking two key steps. First of all, they have learned more about their own family structure and relationships. Second, they have found they are able to take practical steps to adjust those relationships.

Remember: the ultimate goal for all families is both to put down roots of self-worth and to grow in independence and competence. The devoted family provides plenty of roots. But when love begins to smother, the wings get clipped.

Part II

# HOW PARENTS BECOME OVERINVOLVED

# Chapter 5

# GOOD REASONS FOR BAD RESULTS

Over the years, I've heard a wide variety of feelings and motivations expressed by parents who were concerned about doing the right things for their children.

"My parents were so cold and harsh. I swore I wasn't going to be like that with my children!"

"You think I do a lot for my kids? You ought to meet my mother!"

"John was away so much. When he did come home, he was exhausted. So I always tried to make up for that by doing all I could for the kids."

"I used to be so lonely sitting at home with no one to talk to. Bob was either out drinking or riveted to the TV. Since we've had the children, I've had something to keep me busy. Now, I talk more to the kids than to my own husband!"

"If I say white, my husband will say black. Whatever I say, he disagrees. At least my daughter usually sees things my way. But my son always seems to stick up for his dad. So I guess we have an even match in our house."

"I feel bad being away from my boys all day working,

so I try to make up for it when I get home. But sometimes, I think I let them get away with too much.''

"Sarah takes so long and makes such a mess when she makes her own sandwich. It's a lot easier just to make it for her.''

The feelings of each of these parents are reasonable and understandable. In my experience of counseling overinvolved parents, I almost always find that there are good reasons for their natural love to become a more stifling, dependent love.

## Reason #1:
## Parents Learn From Grandparents

Every daughter learns most of what she knows about mothering from her parents. Although there are many books and other resources available on parenting, few parents have any formal training in this skill. Even if you happen to have formal training, what you learned from your own parents will undoubtedly carry more weight than any skills or understanding you acquired in a classroom.

In general, the lessons learned from grandparents can take two forms in overinvolved families. The first is that parents may learn to repeat for their own children the smothering that they received from their parents. The second lesson is that parents may smother their own kids in their efforts to avoid or react against the neglect that they themselves encountered at home.

### REPEATING THE SMOTHERING PATTERN

One mother I know, a thirty-five-year-old professional woman, had been waited on, hand and foot, all her life by her own mother. As a result, she came to think of loving as "doing for." To show love, her mother couldn't just say, "I love you," or sit quietly in the presence of the loved one, or encourage the child's independent activities. Instead, she always had to be up and about, physically assisting, choosing clothes, driving family members places, reminding, nagging, and picking up after.

The daughter had been trained so well in this type of "love" that it was natural—indeed, practically inevitable—that she would try to do at least as much for her own children. In fact, this daughter tried to outdo her mother's example when she began to deal with her own children.

If the mother had given occasional advice, the daughter would give constant advice. If the mother had occasionally helped the child choose or buy her clothes, the daughter would always do it for her children. The daughter loved her mother and wanted to love her own children just as much, but she showed that love by "doing for." In short, this daughter had learned all too well from her own mother—so well that her actions produced a disabling, Dependent Love Pattern in her children.

As we consider the roles of an individual mother or daughter in such a situation, it's important not to resort to blaming anyone. Remember: the young mother who was going overboard in this situation was *also* a daughter, who had learned a variety of lessons from her mom and dad. And her mom was also a daughter. Relationships in families are a great web, with no individual person being at fault. We must look at these situations positively, as family relationships where everyone has the opportunity to change.

## REACTING AGAINST NEGLECT

The daughter who becomes a smothering mother may have learned her overinvolvement not from a smothering mother, but from one who was neglectful. One young woman indicated to me that she felt she had been neglected throughout her childhood. Neither her father nor her mother had shown her the warmth or affection she felt she had deserved.

Among other things, she felt her parents had saddled her with too much responsibility at too early an age. She always seemed to be working around the house when other girls her age were out participating in school activities or just socializing with one another. She felt that her parents had not given her the attention she deserved on birthdays and other special occasions. Somehow, these personal milestones passed without any parties and with few presents.

Having felt this neglect and lack of involvement from her mother and father, this daughter was determined that things would be different with her own children. As a result, she became extremely attentive to the needs of her young son and daughter. She catered to their every whim and frequently bought them anything they asked for in the store. She rarely used babysitters and never established a set schedule of responsibilities or chores for her children. In other words, in an heroic effort to avoid neglect, she flipped to the other extreme and began to become overinvolved and smothering in her children's lives.

When we first talked, this young woman indicated she was determined not to allow her own children to experience the same hands-off childhood that she had known. But as we went further into our discussions, she began to reconsider. She started to understand that her approach to her children was not something that she had thought through thoroughly, as much as it was a behavioral reaction to her own neglected childhood. In the course of our conversations, I drew an analogy this way: "Your situation is similar to what happens to a person who is hit from the right side in a car accident. From then on, she's very careful to check the right side of the street, the right side of cars, the right side of everything—so much so, that she completely ignores any danger from the left!"

In short, parenting requires a balanced approach, one that is neither smothering nor neglectful. Simply determining to be different from your parents—without a careful assessment of exactly what you should do and how you should resolve an angry relationship with them—can result in the exact opposite of what you intend. When this woman finally understood this principle, she developed an ability to love not by simply being constantly attentive, but by encouraging her children to develop independence and responsibility.

### LEARNING TO SMOTHER FROM YOUR CULTURE

The lessons that parents learn from grandparents may come from strong cultural expectations. Of course, individual families within a culture differ, so generalizations are impossible. But certain cultures do, more frequently than others, foster devoted families with the strengths of loyalty, expressiveness, and emotional warmth. Yet along with these strengths comes the danger of overinvolvement, where loving becomes smothering concern.

There's also a peculiar problem that may develop with second- or third-generation children whose parents or grandparents come from a culture that emphasizes the importance of the devoted family. The parents may stress love and family devotion in their relationships with the children, perhaps even more than their parents did, in an effort to hold onto their cultural values in a new land. On the other hand, the children's peers in the new American culture often emphasize personal choice and independence.

This conflict between (1) the devoted family emphasis at home and (2) the independent emphasis at school or on the playground often begins at a very early age and intensifies as the child grows older. I'm reminded of one very close family that moved to New York from Ecuador. The eldest daughter in this family developed a very strong sense of responsibility toward her parents and siblings over the years, primarily as a result of a cultural emphasis on the importance of family loyalty and devotion. She was, in effect, expected to be a kind of "second mother" in the family, as she helped her mom do various house-keeping tasks and also take care of the younger children.

As it happened, this young woman was also extremely bright and ambitious, so she fit right into her new American culture and became quite popular throughout her high school and college years. She did extremely well in her classwork, graduated near the top of her class in both high school and college, and went on to a highly successful career in advertising.

But even as she was achieving the American Dream in many ways, she constantly felt the tug from her family and her Hispanic culture. Her parents, who did not understand what was going on inside their daughter, constantly demanded that she spend time at the family house. They insisted that their daughter continue to help out with family responsibilities—even though she was attempting to carry on a high-powered career at the same time. In effect, this young woman felt pressure to be two people: the dutiful Latin American daughter, and the hard-charging young American career woman.

Obviously, something had to give in this situation. Finally, the young woman, feeling "wrung out" and "pressured beyond belief," to use her words, came to me for help.

"I don't know what to do because I just can't seem to get my life in order," she said. "I know what I'm *supposed* to do, but I just don't have time to do it! I don't even have time to date anybody. Yet my mother keeps telling me I'd better hurry up and meet somebody and get married before I'm too old!"

This young woman was following her cultural values of loyalty and obedience not only to her parents and their requests, but also to her job and its demands. Trying to please everyone had left her worn ragged, and feeling torn in two. She had not learned how to make her own decisions and blend together the values she most treasured as an independent adult.

Through our counseling she learned to look at various possibilities and choose her priorities, rather than simply respond dutifully to all requests. She came to realize she could never fulfill all her parents' expectations or fit the pattern of their culture. At the same time, she didn't want to reject the strengths of her cultural background, such as the deep family commitment and caring.

She resolved her conflict by telling her parents that she could no longer stop by every evening after work. But she did try to make it every Sunday for the big family dinner—to which she brought flowers for her mother and a paper for her father.

Although this young woman wanted to have a successful career, she also realized she had been sacrificing her own peer relationships. She began setting aside one evening a week to go out with friends. In fact, she told her boss she had to leave early every Wednesday.

She even began dating—a decision that pleased her mother. Her increased interest in men made her parents willing to lessen their demands on her.

As a result of these changes, she began to enjoy both her parents and her job more by limiting what she could do with each. She developed a sense of herself apart from what others expected of her, a self that was its own wonderful blend of caring for others and independent thinking.

Another key factor besides cultural inheritances in smothering overinvolvement by a mother may be a father who is emotionally distant from other family members.

### Reason #2:
### Distant Fathers May Encourage
### Overinvolved Mothers

Because every child has both a mother and a father, whenever I am consulted about a child's problem, I ask to speak with both parents. Often a mother may say, speaking softly, so the child doesn't hear, "Her father's not really a part of our life," or "His father is very busy. I'll have to take care of this." But these dismissed or excused fathers are in fact a vital part of understanding and resolving the difficulties.

For example, when a mother is smothering a child, you can be certain that in most cases there's a distant father in the background. In other words, Dad remains separated from the other family members by avoiding emotional or physical interactions. Yet the distant father has a big impact on family relationships. In fact, his very lack of involvement often encourages the mother to become overinvolved.

What makes many fathers distant figures in their own families? There are a number of causes. Sometimes, of course, as a result of such factors as divorce or death, a father may not be present at all in a family. We'll deal in detail with such situations a little later. But dads who are around may often be separated in terms of three types of distance: emotional distance, alcoholic or drug related distance, and handicapped distance.

## EMOTIONAL DISTANCE

Often, fathers are emotionally distant because that's the way they were taught to behave when they were children in their original families. Their own fathers may have provided financially for the family and assumed that was where their responsibilities ended. The son, when he became a father, looked at this role model and figured, "Well, if *my* dad did it that way, then why shouldn't I?"

Sometimes, the emotionally distant father may feel that he's actually "gone the extra mile" in doing more than is expected of him by his family. He may spend a little extra time with the children or perhaps take everybody out to dinner. Then, he'll say to himself, "I certainly do better than old Joe down the block, who *never* spends any time with his kids!"

In fact, such a father may recall that his own father was never around at all when he was growing up. So the son who has become a father may feel he's doing quite well just being physically present and providing financially for the family.

Because many fathers spend relatively little time with their children, mothers who are concerned about bringing youngsters up the right way may try to make up for this distance by becoming overinvolved. These smothering moms sometimes go overboard in showing concern and attention for their kids without suggesting or insisting that Dad participate more in child rearing. Instead, they often assume that a distant father just reflects the way life is. They've seen their own fathers and many other men operate in the same way as their husbands. So they say, ''There's just so much you can expect from a man!''

But in fact, I think that we expect far too little from fathers. Even as we ask so little from them, we often blame mothers for being too attentive. The final result of all this is that fathers lose out on the challenge and joy of parenting responsibilities and mothers are overburdened. As a result, devoted families are thrown out of balance. Unfortunately, the ones who suffer most from the imbalance are the children, who may fail to develop independent adult coping skills as they become enmeshed in a Dependent Love Pattern.

The absent father may begin as an absent husband. Sure, he may be *physically* present. In fact, he may be quite demanding, in a physical sense. He wants his dinner served on time; he wants the house spotless; he wants the children kept out of his hair while he's reading the paper, watching TV, or otherwise relaxing; and he wants a sexually available wife. But beyond the financial, he's never learned how to give to others in the family and share in their burdens and sorrows. He often doesn't understand how important it is to ask his wife how her day went. He doesn't understand how much she appreciates occasional flowers, small gifts, and hand-holding and hugging. Certainly, he doesn't have the time or the inclination to sit down for long talks on her personal concerns or family problems.

In many cases, as I've said, distant fathers may come from families where their fathers didn't know how to give or share emotionally. In that context, the father may have learned certain responses and coping skills, such as "playing dumb." In other words, he may pretend he can't quite figure his wife out when she seems to be worried about something or otherwise out of sorts. Men who have assumed a distant role in their families may often caricature their wives in some way. For example, they may stereotype the wife as the nagging or overly demanding spouse we see on TV sitcoms or in comic strips.

There is a certain selfishness and insularity built into all this. Many fathers have a definite, though rather limited, idea of what's expected of them in their families. This usually includes working all day at the office, earning enough money to keep the family afloat, and occasionally interacting with the kids. More often than not, the main place where these men touch base with their wives is in the bedroom.

A father with such attitudes usually simply can't understand why his wife expects him to do more at home. Besides, when he does contribute something around the house, she never seems satisfied. The more rope he gives her, the more she takes. If he's not careful, she may actually demand that he become an equal partner with her in doing the domestic chores!

Of course, just as absent fathers often begin as absent husbands, so overinvolved mothers often begin as overinvolved wives. For example, a wife may want her husband to listen to her and be with her almost every moment. She may try to cater to her husband's every need but expect equally perfect responses in return. She may look to her husband to make up for all her earlier unmet emotional needs. This attitude on the part of a wife often results in a husband's distancing himself to satisfy his need for more individual space.

After children are born, the wife may turn to them for emotional satisfaction. She may become so absorbed with her offspring that she in effect pushes her husband away. A wife of this type, for instance, may not want to leave children with a babysitter so that she can go out with her husband. Or she may welcome the children into the parents' bed so that sexual relations become impossible.

I often find that such husbands and wives were initially attracted to each other because of the very qualities they later complain about. One wife from an overly involved family was drawn to her husband's independence, sense of security, and ability to speak for himself. The husband, having grown up without a lot of warmth and closeness, was attracted to his wife's warm, talkative, affectionate nature.

But over the years of marriage, they didn't learn to understand and blend their different talents and qualities. Instead, their differences became areas for terrible conflict. With help, however, they began to learn to appreciate each other anew—and balance their respective strengths and weaknesses in more constructive ways.

Spouses who wait a few years to have children—and in the interim, work hard at developing a solid marital relationship—may be better at avoiding some of these conflicts than those who have children right away. But in any case, when the babies do arrive, there will be less time for the husband and wife to interact and build their own relationship. Those couples who have not learned to communicate and share their feelings will be much more likely to slip into a destructive smothering-mother, distant-father pattern.

As the household duties increase with a growing family, the husband may even subtly encourage his wife to become overinvolved with the children. For example, he may compliment her on how well she handles the household and children. In this way, he won't have to deal with extra domestic responsibilities. Also, he may push his wife toward the children so that he doesn't have to deal with her needs for closeness, companionship, or conversation. The wife, for her part, will always see or sense that her husband is becoming less and less available to her. So she may make up for his emotional or physical absence by becoming overinvolved with the children.

Sometimes, a mother who is feeling especially frustrated because of her bad relationship with her husband may start enthusiastically to share confidences with her sons and daughters. She may vent all her unhappiness into the ear of a favorite youngster and may become more involved in trying to control the child's life. As a result, the child will become more dependent on the mother and may well find later that he or she is ill-prepared for the rigors of an independent, successful life in the adult world. The child may not be able to bear the guilt of quitting the job of confidant to develop intimate peer relationships.

One fifty-two-year-old mother, Virginia, had been married to her husband, Will, for many years. But she was feeling tremendously depressed and unhappy about the relationship. Among other things, she was suffering from insomnia, always felt tired, and in general sensed that her life lacked purpose.

As we talked, it became apparent that one reason for her emotional anguish was the fact that both her children had moved out of the house and were now living in other parts of the country. Her son had embarked on a career in business and had already begun his own family. Her daughter, Sally, had completed her MBA and was involved in a management training program in a large corporation.

With the children gone, Virginia felt her life no longer had much meaning. In effect, she was out of her main job, because over the past two decades she had devoted practically every waking hour to rearing her youngsters.

At the same time, she and Will had grown farther and farther apart.

Actually, this husband and wife had never been very close, even from the beginning of their marriage. Will was an almost classic example of the emotionally distant husband and father. He provided well for his family, did occasional favors for his wife, saw his children for a few minutes each day, and in this way felt that he had met all his obligations.

The couple's two children had come early, after Will and Virginia had been married only a year or so. As a result, neither spouse had gotten to know the other very well. With the arrival of the first baby, Virginia threw herself into being an attentive mother, and that suited Will just fine. He was not one who liked to talk about his feelings or get involved in sticky emotional issues. With his wife occupied in child rearing, he focused on what he regarded as his main family responsibilities, which included earning a living and doing a few handyman chores around the house. Then, he spent his extra time playing cards or going to sports events with some of his buddies.

One of the things that distressed and puzzled Virginia was that there was very little she could point to, either in her marriage or any other aspect of her family life, that she had to complain about. As far as she knew, Will had always been faithful to her, and he did about as much around the house as any other husband she knew. They rarely even argued about anything.

On the other hand, there was something seriously wrong about the way Virginia was feeling, both physically and emotionally. Virginia noticed that their daughter, Sally, also seemed to be generally unhappy as she wrestled with a variety of emotional problems. When even little things went wrong in Sally's life, or when she had a minor decision to make or personal difficulty to deal with, she would experience terrible anxiety. An ulcer and frequent migraines were telltale signs of her internal churning.

As a result, Sally and Virginia were frequently on the phone talking in minute detail about Sally's life. Virginia even made several trips out to the city where Sally was working in order to provide her daughter with advice and support.

"I've tried to do my best with my family, but somehow, everything seems to be going wrong!" Virginia told me. "Where did I mess up?"

In fact, as I told her, she hadn't "messed up." Instead, her family relationships, which were basically quite lovingly oriented, had become unbalanced. To set things right, it would be necessary not only for Virginia, but also for her husband and their children, to become involved in correcting the imbalance.

Although Virginia was sure that her husband would never come in to join her for the therapy sessions, he turned out to be willing to cooperate, once he realized the importance of his participation. Consequently, I saw the two of them for nearly a year. Our focus during that entire time was on building channels of communication between husband and wife—channels that they had never developed earlier in their marriage.

Among other things, I encouraged Virginia to concentrate on listening and showing affection without talking. She had always tended to be a chatterbox, around both her husband and her children. As a result, she sometimes overlooked other ways of showing her feelings and affections.

As for Will, I encouraged him to talk more and to gain her attention by looking at her directly and taking her hand. Because he was just learning the rudiments of establishing an intimate husband–wife relationship, I kept much of my advice simple. I told him that he should concentrate on four key responses to his wife, depending on the problem or issue she brought up with him.

In the first place, if he had done something wrong, he

should say, "I'm sorry," without qualifying his apology in any way. Believe it or not, he had never actually said these words to his wife. Second, if she did something for him—even something very small—he should always say, "Thank you." Although this may sound routine, it's a simple practice that's underused and produces dramatic results.

Third, he should look for something every day to compliment his wife on. For example, if her hair looked better than normal, he should say, "Your hair looks great today!" Finally, he agreed to give his wife at least one small token of his appreciation every week. This might be a card, flowers, or an invitation to go to a movie. Although these may sound overly simple, I'm often surprised that many men really don't know how important they are. And I'm amazed at how many couples see dramatic improvement when they actually use these well-known expressions of love.

Once Virginia and Will were on a more productive track in their interactions, they were in a better position to deal more effectively with their children. Among other things, Will started advising Sally when she called, rather than leaving that responsibility to his wife alone. He even initiated calls from time to time, a previously unheard-of practice. Virginia, though it took a strong act of will, avoided getting so involved with Sally and encouraged her to reach out to friends. Instead, she focused on developing her own new activities. She began volunteering at a day care center and joined a women's bridge club.

This better balance in family relationships, with the father taking a more assertive role, helped Sally start to become more independent. Apparently, more than either parent had realized, their daughter had desperately needed her father's emotional involvement in her life. She had in addition worried anxiously about her mother's loneliness.

Often, such problems may go unrecognized in loving and devoted families until emotional difficulties emerge in either the children or the parents. In this case, both the mother and one of her children had problems— problems that were deep internal cries for help.

It's fortunate when the parents in such families are strong enough and mature enough to deal directly with their own relationship. Often, when Mom and Dad work out their own problems, they're in a much better position to free their children to become more independent. But sometimes, when parents can't quite get things right between themselves, the children will continue to pay the emotional price—as happens when alcoholism enters the devoted family scene.

## ALCOHOL OR DRUG-INDUCED DISTANCE

In some families, alcohol or drugs may place a barrier between the father and the rest of the family. Dad may often seem quite gregarious and involved with his wife and children. But when he drinks, he may quickly become irresponsible, undependable, or uncommunicative. The fact that his drinking may not be predictable can add further to the tension in the family and the feelings of distance from Dad.

Many times, a smothering mother and children with emotional difficulties may act as convenient smoke screens for the more serious illness of alcoholism—which no one in the family is willing to admit. As long as the mother compensates for the father and the father doesn't regularly make a public spectacle of himself, everyone in the family may pretend that they're living normal lives. But in fact, the mother's worry about the father and consequent overinvolvement with her children may be taking all her energy and setting her up for her own emotional problems.

The children may get into the habit of being very secretive about their father's illness. If they talk to anyone about it, that confidante will usually be the mother. Unfortunately the more the mother and the children engage in such emotionally charged confidences, the more interdependent the relationship between the mother and children may become.

I'll often find that when families of this type come in looking for help with the children's problems, it quickly becomes evident that the *real* problem is the drinking, or sometimes drug use. But unfortunately, in some cases, if I even hint that we should focus on the drinking rather than on other difficulties in the family, the entire family may stop their therapy sessions. Nobody is willing to blow the whistle on Dad. Everyone has gotten so used to hiding, and, in effect, supporting his drinking habit that they're fearful of what may happen if they begin to rock the boat.

Rebecca and Kyle were a typical couple who confronted such a drinking problem. Rebecca was naturally a very loving woman, and for that matter, Kyle had always been a fairly easygoing, warm person. But Kyle had been wrestling with a sense of inferiority all his life, and he had a family history of alcoholism. When life's frustrations and worries arose, it was tempting for him to find solace in the local bar or in one of the liquor bottles he kept hidden in a closet. Kyle explained that drinking "occasionally," as he put it, helped him to relax and get over his worries. But in fact, Kyle drank quite often and frequently either came home drunk or drank himself into a stupor in front of the television set.

Rebecca became increasingly frustrated and angry at Kyle's emotional absence and drinking. She also became extremely concerned about Kyle's health, because medical checkups showed he was developing heart and liver problems. She harbored deep fears for the future of her family. As a result, she developed serious headaches and backaches, which sometimes made it very difficult for her even to get out of bed in the morning.

Occasionally, Rebecca tried to engage Kyle in a conversation about his drinking, in the hope that she might be able to get him to cut back on it. He interpreted her overtures as "nagging" or "meddling," and invariably, after she approached him in this way, he would retreat even more deeply into his bottle. In short, his drinking problem and their inability to communicate about it triggered an ongoing, ever-deepening cycle of alcoholic distance, which separated Kyle from the rest of the family.

Finally, when their two children reached their twenties, both continued to live at home because they felt "Mom needed them." It became evident that something had to be done about the situation.

During counseling, all the family members realized that the two children had become overly dependent on their mother, at least partly in response to their father's drinking habit. Kyle's drinking had separated him emotionally from the others, and to make up for his absence Rebecca had thrown herself into excessive involvement in the lives of her son and daughter. Consequently, the children continued to depend on her to take care of them in many areas that they actually should have been handling themselves.

Both children were worried about their father and devoted to their mother, who they thought needed their shoulders to lean on when Dad began one of his drinking bouts. In fact, they had become their mother's confidants concerning the father's problem. They all regularly discussed Kyle and vainly attempted to set up strategies to discourage him from drinking. Sometimes, one of the children would hide the bottles or throw them away. At other times, the son or daughter would confront Kyle in a harsh argument. But none of these tactics worked.

Finally, as a result of the counseling experience, the family members began to work more constructively with one another to adjust their difficult situation. First of all, Kyle and Rebecca took the difficult step of working on the serious problems in their marriage. Rebecca began to confront Kyle's drinking rather than turn to the children. Kyle faced up to the destructiveness of his drinking and finally, after a near-disaster while driving one night, began to attend Alcoholics Anonymous. The children began to focus on their own friendships and job goals. They made plans to move out into their own apartments—as they well could do, as one held a good job and the other had several job prospects.

It takes great courage to face up to the real issue of alcoholism in any family. Even with all the recent publicity about celebrities and others who have become involved with alcohol and drug abuse, many people are still reluctant to acknowledge that they have a problem. Somehow, it's just too demeaning or degrading to say, "I'm an alcoholic," or, "I have a drug-dependency problem."

This reluctance is understandable because in the minds of many people, such problems seem to reflect some sort of character defect or inherent personal flaw. But in fact, alcoholism is an illness that needs recognition and treatment like any other disease before it destroys family relationships.

### HANDICAPPED DISTANCE

Sometimes, a father may find himself separated from his wife and children by a physical or emotional handicap. Families may exaggerate or focus on the ways a handicap keeps a parent from being fully capable, rather than on overcoming it by developing the disabled person's involvement in the family.

A father who is confined to a wheelchair will probably find that he simply can't interact with his sons and daughters on an athletic playing field in the same way as a father without a handicap. The family can use this to make him a distant dad, or they can overcome it by helping him experience greater involvement in the children's other interests. Similarly, a father with a mental problem may be seen as someone to shy away from or to be shielded from others, or he can become more of an equal partner who can function up to his personal potential in family activities.

No handicap in itself disqualifies a man or woman as

a parent. It's just necessary for these special parents and their loved ones to adjust their activities and relationships so as to maximize the handicapped parent's strengths in participating with the children and spouse.

One father, who had become a quadriplegic as a result of a car accident, could talk and think normally. He just couldn't use his arms or legs and was dependent on others to push him around in a wheelchair. As a result, he began to feel that he was really of no use around the home, and his wife, feeling sorry for him, played into this attitude by shielding him from any household responsibilities. She chose to shoulder all the discipline and other child-rearing duties, including helping the kids with their homework.

As a result of this mother's overinvolvement with her children, her young son and daughter began to depend on her far too much and frequently fell into baby-like roles with her. Her eleven-year-old boy, for example, would crawl into bed with her almost every night. He claimed that he was afraid of the dark and couldn't stay asleep unless he spent part of the night with her. This mother did many things for the boy and his seven-year-old sister that they should have been doing for themselves. For example, she took on all the responsibilities of cleaning up their rooms and never asked them to help out with family chores, such as taking care of the lawn or clearing the dinner table.

After this woman and her husband explored their situation in several therapy sessions, both realized that the husband could be doing a great deal more with the children. In particular, he was quite capable of shouldering some of the discipline responsibilities. Even though he was unable to leave his wheelchair, he still had a commanding voice, and both children seemed to welcome his corrections and admonitions when they had done something wrong. Being a very bright person, he was also in a good position to help the children with their homework.

As the father began to contribute more of his presence

and support, the family became more balanced, with both parents participating more evenly in the child rearing. New lines of communication also opened up between husband and wife. Perhaps most important of all, the children began to take on more responsibilities, such as making their own lunches and doing yard work. The son stopped sleeping in his mother's bed; and in general, both youngsters became much more self-assured and independent.

From these illustrations, you can see that a distant father can play a crucial role in encouraging smothering by a mother. That's why an emotionally distant father is one good reason for the interactions in a devoted family to become distorted and lead to problems. But now, let's turn to another important reason for a Dependent Love Pattern—parental conflicts.

### Reason #3:
### Parents May Pull Children
### Into Their Conflicts

When a mother and father start fighting, children are often caught in the middle. Unfortunately, parents may think children should know about their particular complaints and concerns against the other spouse.

Why do parents sometimes feel this way? For one thing, a parent may want to justify his own position in the conflict. Or he may feel he needs a child as a confidant, as no one else is available. Or the parent may want to help the youngster avoid later on the negative qualities that the parent feels characterize the mate.

Unfortunately, though, as parents pull their children into their adult conflicts, the youngsters may end up taking on the worst qualities of each parent, rather than the best. Children who are forced into the middle like this may find themselves being pulled apart emotionally.

In one family the husband and wife stayed together,

but they fought constantly. Too often, they tried to play their son off against one another.

The mother would pamper the boy and even encourage him to stay home from school on the slightest whim. The father, in contrast, would frequently criticize the mother in the son's presence by saying, "You know, your mother's not very smart." Or, "Your mother's a very unsophisticated woman—and I certainly hope you won't pick up her weaknesses."

Feeling constantly tugged back and forth, this boy experienced tremendous guilt and uncertainty as he sided with one parent on one occasion, and then the other on another occasion, in his natural love for both parents. Sometimes, he listened closely to what his father was saying about his mother, and then joined Dad in making fun of her. But afterward, the boy would be racked with remorse because he felt that he had been disloyal. On the other hand, as he grew older, he had the distinct impression that he had been too much of a "momma's boy" as a youngster. So he found himself wishing he had developed a better relationship with his father.

This man grew up feeling loved by both parents, but emotionally torn apart by their conflicts. It took years of therapy and hard work at his relationships for him to gain more of a sense of confidence and independence. Only then could he move toward a better relationship with each parent.

Sometimes, one parent may become so close to a child in these conflicts that the parent in effect overconnects with the child. The child, in an emotional sense, may even seem to become the parent's substitute spouse.

In one situation I encountered, the mother and father were constantly fighting with one another. They brought their daughter into these conflicts, but on those occasions when the girl sided with her mother, the father became enraged. One time, his anger became so intense that the father yelled at the daughter: "If that's the way you feel, you can just get out of this house!"

The daughter, who was in her late teens at the time, decided she had had enough, so she *did* leave. But then her mother left with her! In fact, the mother and daughter eventually set up housekeeping together.

These family members were able to repair their relationships only after both of the parents and the child sat down, discussed the matter, and realized that they had allowed their conflicts to get completely out of hand. Eventually, the mother acknowledged that she had, in effect, turned her daughter into a kind of surrogate husband, who actually got a higher priority in her mind than her real husband.

If the mother and daughter had continued along this track, each would have become so dependent on the other that neither would have been able to lead a truly free and autonomous life in the future. Both parents and the daughter were especially concerned because the daughter's social life had deteriorated considerably after she and her mother had moved in together. Fortunately, the husband and wife in this family got back together again in the family home, and the daughter moved into her own apartment with a roommate her own age.

In other family conflicts, children may remain in a dependent, childlike role even after they become adults. Sometimes, they secretly fear that if they grow up and move away from home, their parents' conflicts will become so severe that the marriage will fall apart. The children see themselves as the necessary "glue" that holds the marriage together. As a result, they in effect sacrifice their own lives for the parents' relationship. They must remain children in order to keep the family status quo.

To escape such a dependency pattern, both parents and children must recognize what's going on and begin to take decisive steps to adjust their relationships. Children in these enmeshed families need to realize clearly that they are neither responsible for their parents' problems nor are they able to solve them. The health of a marriage is entirely up to the husband and wife. The spouses started their relationship long before children arrived, and they have a relationship as a couple separate from their role as parents. They alone can decide what shape and direction it will take.

Children must acknowledge that their parents are grownups who must deal with their own conflicts, without the help or presence of the child. If Mom and Dad, as adults, have difficulty resolving their mutual problems, then a child certainly cannot do it for them.

Finally, caring mothers who go through a divorce may inadvertently fall into the trap of encouraging their children to become more dependent on them. Emotional trauma and bad feelings often accompany divorce suits. A mother who has custody of her children may be plagued by guilt and worry over the possible effect of separation on the children. She knows the divorce has been hard on them, and so she tries to make up for it.

In one such case, the mother began to treat her son as her best friend. She needed someone to confide in and share her emotions with when she came home from work. So she turned to her ten-year-old boy, who was both articulate and sensitive to his mother's needs. Unfortunately, this extra attention from his mother made him increasingly dependent on her, and also made her increasingly dependent on him.

In addition to unloading her own worries on the boy, the mother usually questioned him in detail after he had paid a visit to his father. She still felt strong ties to her former husband, and she hoped that somehow they might be able to get back together again. She always wanted to know whether her former husband was happy and whether or not he was dating other women.

In effect, then, this boy became his mother's confidant and main companion—and also her spy, who brought back information regularly on his father. As a result, he soon found that a good portion of his life was tied up in dealing with his parents' emotions and conflicts. This excessive family involvement left him little time or emotional energy to develop solid peer friendships of his own. His preoccupation with his parents' problems distracted him from his schoolwork and the ordinary outside activities that boys of his age pursued.

As this boy grew older, he began to resent his parents' intrusion into his personal time and activities. Eventually, he became so frustrated with their interactions—and the way they played him off against one another—that he began trying drugs and getting into trouble at school.

Because of her great care for her son, this mother worked hard to change this pattern. She stopped looking to him as a supporter and looked instead to several friends whom she had not really kept up with as closely as she might have. She stopped asking him about his father and began to support him in his own independent activities and interests.

The son started to realize he was not really the best confidant for his mother and began refusing to be pulled into personal confidences by either his father or his mother. When he understood that his role as mediator was doomed to failure, he decided to devote his energies to more productive pursuits, like his own friendships and career.

Of course, all husbands and wives have differences. And few couples make it through a relationship that lasts for years, decades, or a lifetime without some serious disagreements. The point is not to deny these differences, nor to avoid all conflict. In fact, a healthy approach to fighting is a skill all couples need to develop.

But parents must avoid pulling children into the middle of marital conflicts. When children are exposed and pulled into marital fights on any regular basis, they are certain to develop insecurities, anxieties, and difficulty in moving ahead with their own life tasks. Children can be spared this damage if parents stop seeking children's opinions and support for their side, and instead deal directly with each other in discussing, debating, and working out creative solutions to their problems. For heated and lengthy disagreements, one way of protecting children is to find a time and place to hash things out alone.

## Reason #4:
## Special Circumstances May Promote
## Parental Overinvolvement

As we've seen, mothers are programmed in our society to try to do and be everything for their children. Those moms operating out of devoted families may feel especially burdened by a need to show love and concern toward their children—no matter what obstacles they face. Yet in many cases, the roadblocks may be so formidable that mothers become unusually inclined to overcompensate by smothering their children emotionally.

Some of the special circumstances that may promote parental overinvolvement include (1) experiencing divorce or the death of a spouse, (2) being a working mother, (3) having a handicapped child, and (4) interacting with an only child or the youngest child. Each of these situations presents a mother with special challenges as she tries to do her best to love her children, as well as encourage them to become independent and competent as adults.

### THE SINGLE PARENT

As we've already seen, children who are caught in parental conflict as a result of divorce may be trapped in a Dependent Love Pattern. But there are also other ways that children of single parents may run into problems. For example, after a divorce that involves minimal conflict or after the death of one parent, a child and a single parent may be thrust together in circumstances that greatly increase the risk of dependent relationships.

In about 90 percent of all single-parent homes, it's the mother who is left with all the responsibilities of child rearing. In such situations, the mother often lacks adequate emotional, financial, or physical resources to do the job that she feels she should do. Some mothers feel guilty and try to make up for this by overinvolvement.

Those mothers who find success and even enjoyment in this difficult situation usually have accepted one important fact: they can't be two parents. They can never make up for the fact that the child doesn't have a father. They give up the inappropriate guilt and instead find ways to obtain extra support for both themselves and their children.

These effective single mothers also realize that their main job is not to protect their children from the cold, cruel world, or to pamper their youngsters to compensate for their extra hardships. Rather, the single mother's job is to equip her children to live responsibly in the real world, just as the mother herself has learned to live responsibly.

Single mothers must give their youngsters a foundation of love, but also encourage the children every step of the way to learn to care for themselves. Children must be taught how to make friends, how to handle friends' questions about their family, how to make their own decisions, and how to execute various chores and tasks successfully.

In other words, the mother and the child confront this single-parenting situation together—but not with a child acting as a co-parent. The youngster must develop a feeling of security in his role as a responsible child, a role that gradually moves him toward mature adulthood.

## THe WORKING MOTHER

At one time or another, all working mothers become overburdened. They work all day at the office and then, when they arrive at home, they're expected to give their all to household and child-care tasks. Unfortunately, as we've already seen, many fathers in our culture don't carry an equal load in caring for the home or children, in part because no one expects the father to do as much as the mother.

But this kind of arrangement, with the mother working full time and yet also taking primary responsibility for the house and children, is tailor-made to wear a woman out. When the mother is operating virtually alone in taking care of her children, it's easy for her to give in to her child's immature, irresponsible behavior. There's a tendency to excuse her youngsters' foibles or misbehavior because she fears, down deep, that maybe she hasn't been as available to her children as she should have been. Working mothers often feel somewhat guilty that they haven't spent more time with their children. So, when they are with their youngsters, such mothers may be more permissive and do more for their children than they would if they were with them all day long.

Speaking for myself, I know that I tend to tolerate more irresponsible behavior from my own children when I've been away at work during the day than when I've been at home. Why do I react this way? When I've been away, I want to compensate by spending extra time with them and giving lots of love. In a sense, I want to make up for having been away from my children.

But I've come to realize that my children just do not benefit from parental indulgence of their whining or failure to finish their daily chores. What they need most is loving but firm encouragement to get their responsibilities finished, and to stop whining. After I've been firm on these matters, my expressions of affection come across as genuine love, rather than as permissiveness.

It's easy for working mothers to lose perspective on what constitutes good behavior and what doesn't. Actions that mothers may see as cute when they haven't been around the child all day may actually be the same behavior that produces bad conduct grades or turns off friends at school. Certainly, in the relatively short time that a working mother is with her children at home, she needs to devote a great deal of attention and love to her child. There has to be plenty of "quality time" in which the mother and child interact and communicate on a relatively intense level. But at the same time, a *complete* demonstration of love will involve teaching the child the proper limits to his behavior, as well as a sense of responsibility.

Implicit in these observations is this important principle: your tendency to be smothering or harsh toward your children is usually not related directly to whether or not you work. In other words, it's unfair to assume that just because you work, you won't smother your youngster, get overinvolved, or fail to teach responsibility.

Smothering doesn't depend so much on the amount of contact with your child as it does on your way of relating. You can apply a smothering approach twelve hours a day or one hour a day. Similarly, you can be harsh or unloving twelve hours a day or one hour a day. Working mothers just face a special challenge: they must not allow the limited time they spend with their children to make them feel so guilty that they fail to encourage their children's independence and responsibility when they are around them.

None of us can be Supermom. It's much more important to provide *appropriate* love in the time and circumstances that we have available. And that includes teaching a sense of responsibility and the basic skills of independence.

## PARENTS OF HANDICAPPED CHILDREN

With a handicapped child, parents sometimes tend to go overboard in doing things for the youngster in an effort to make up for the physical or mental disability. And certainly, handicapped youngsters do require a great deal of love because dealing with physical or mental problems is no easy matter for anyone, much less a child.

But I've discovered that it's often doubly important for the handicapped child to gain a sense of competence, because throughout his life, many people are going to focus on what he *can't* do rather than on what he can do. The most natural thing may be to baby a disabled child

or tolerate his immature behavior. But unless you treat
your child as normally as possible and give him as much
personal responsibility as he can bear, the extra support
that you think you're giving him may in fact cripple him
further.

I always urge parents of handicapped children to give
lots of appropriate love, but also to encourage solid
growth. In other words, I tell them to emphasize, even
more than they would with a normal child, what the child
*can* do, and to compliment his or her strengths fully:
"You're so good at math!" Or, "What a great athlete
you are!" Or, "If you keep working hard at this, you're
going to get a great job!"

Another danger of treating your handicapped child differently from other children is that he or she may actually
begin to *feel* different. The child who feels different may
have a lot of trouble fitting in and relating to other children. For that matter, other youngsters in the family or
neighborhood who aren't getting all the extra special attention may begin to feel jealous. As any parent of a
handicapped child knows, the normal balancing act of
not playing favorites with children becomes especially
hard when a handicapped child is part of the equation.

One very loving evangelical Christian family came to
me because their nineteen-year-old son, who was mildly
retarded and had a learning disability, seemed unable to
do much of anything on his own. Interestingly enough,
he had passed his special-ed courses, developed a lot of
friendships, and even held a part-time job while he was
in high school. After graduation, he had gone out and
gotten a job and was developing some independence.

Then, the family moved to another state, and the parents became quite worried. They feared that their son,
who had done so well in the old environment, might not
be able to make a good transition to the new location.
The boy himself expressed many reservations and fears
about making the move, and the parents gave in to his
insecurities. When they moved to the new place, he

wanted to spend all his time at home or with them. As they told me during a counseling session, the boy seemed to shrivel up under these changed circumstances, and they didn't quite know what to do about it.

After we had had several discussions on their family situation, I gave them an okay to be a bit hard on their son. Specifically, I told them first to map out a set of clear-cut responsibilities that he would have to take on around the house. Then, I encouraged them to set target dates and goals to get him out looking for a job in the new community.

Although the boy at first seemed afraid of the new challenges, when he started to accomplish something, he soon perked up and felt proud of himself. He actually began to look forward to the prospect of doing things independently and getting off on his own. In fact, he took a great deal of pride in household and occupational tasks that he had previously insisted were going to be impossible for him in the new environment.

Clearly, then, a handicap doesn't mean that a parent has to pamper a child forever. On the contrary, special children often can exercise more independence and responsibility than we give them credit for. It's just necessary for parents to know their youngster's strengths as well as limits and encourage that special child to travel as far as he can on his own.

## PARENTS DEALING WITH A YOUNGEST CHILD OR ONLY CHILD

A number of researchers have concluded that birth order may have a great influence on important personal characteristics of children. For example, the "baby" in the family, or the youngest child, may be more pampered than the others. In part, this may be because the youngest child is the mother's last baby, and it can be very difficult for her to watch that last one grow up. Also, if the other children have any nurturing tendencies, they may help the mother smother the youngest child.

An only child has many of the same difficulties as the youngest child because he or she represents the parents' only connection with the younger generation, which is now growing into adulthood. With caring, involved parents, an only child receives all of the parental concern, rather than having it shared among several children. If this is overdone, the child may suffer "stunted growth" along with the love.

Parents may apply additional pressure on an only child or a youngest child to be more available to them emotionally and to get involved with them in their activities. However, parents must be careful that their involvement doesn't turn into *over*involvement and help produce a Dependent Love Pattern.

Each of these physical situations can make it more difficult for parents who naturally tend to be loving toward their children to reach a healthy parenting balance. To all such parents, I can only say: Continue to give your youngsters as much positive love as you can, but also, give them responsibilities. And if you're alone, get outside support for yourself and your children.

## Reason #5:
## Enabling Takes Time and Courage

Most parents readily agree that their children need to grow up and do things for themselves, but difficulties may emerge when the time arrives to apply this principle to specific situations in the daily pressures of life. Both mothers and fathers are often tempted to take shortcuts to get things done, rather than take time to encourage their children to develop important skills that will promote independence and adult competence.

In the practical pressures of daily life, parents may find that it seems easier to do things for a child rather than teach the child to do things for himself. There's an old saying, "Give a man a fish, and he'll eat fish for a day. Teach a man to fish, and he'll eat for a lifetime." With children, it may seem much quicker, easier, and less frustrating to give them "a fish" than to teach them how to fish. For example, it's definitely less messy to make a peanut butter and jelly sandwich for a five-year-old than to let the child do it himself. It's less hassle to collect the garbage yourself than to require your child to do it. And it's easier to sew on a button than to teach a teen to sew. But in fact, teaching is the only sure route to genuine independence.

It takes a great deal of patience and dedication to teach another person to do anything. If that other person is a young child, the effort and creativity involved in getting a new point across may be especially great. If you've been doing a particular task for a long time and you're quite good at it, you may be tempted by the knowledge that you're going to be able to act more quickly and efficiently than the child.

But if you do take the shortcut, your child will be the loser. You may not be able to see the long-term costs and benefits of a seemingly difficult, drawn-out lesson you give your child in taking on new responsibilities or exercising certain skills. Believe me, though, there will be plenty of long-term benefits. Furthermore, both you and your child will begin to reap those benefits as he or she approaches adulthood and prepares to embark on an independent life.

Another common—and understandable—reason why parents are reluctant to let children do things on their own is that they want to protect their children from harm. At different stages in their development, it may be important for children to play at the far end of the playground. Or they may want to go briefly out of Mom's line of vision, or climb to the top of the monkeybars, or do a balancing act on top of a fairly high fence. Many loving parents will caution their children with a "Be careful now!" More protective parents will always stay right next to their child and say, "You're not old enough to do that" or "You're going to fall."

Sometimes, of course, these cautionary gestures and words may be absolutely appropriate. But many times, they're not. If parents always stay very close to their children and try to provide an absolutely safe environment for them, where the children never even get a skinned knee or a bruise on the bottom, they may be able to provide a high grade of temporary protection.

Yet such protection is *only* temporary; and having it decreases children's ability to build more permanent protection, such as the ability to assess risks, to solve problems, and to care for themselves. Eventually, unless children are given an opportunity to fall a few times in less dangerous situations, they'll end up trying their wings later in more dangerous circumstances, or they'll find they have no wings at all.

So far, most of what we have said has focused on the overinvolved mother. This is because in a majority of devoted families with a Dependent Love Pattern, it is the mother who typically assumes the overinvolved role, while the father remains relatively distant, emotionally or physically. But there are quite a number of families where the same basic family pattern is played out in different ways. There are devoted families where the fathers are the ones who become overinvolved with the child. Although the dynamic is the same, the players are a bit different.

To get a better idea about what this looks like, let's turn now to some families where the father, either by himself or acting with the mother, has gone too far in protecting and "doing for" his children.

# Chapter 6

# CAN A FATHER BE OVERINVOLVED?

Imagine if you will an adult looking back over his or her childhood and making these complaints:

"My father never allowed me to do anything on my own."

"I was Daddy's princess. He got me anything I wanted and did anything I asked him to do."

"My father always fought my battles for me."

"Dad always insisted on getting so involved in my decisions that I never felt I had a chance to decide anything on my own."

"My mother was a very distant figure in our family—but Dad was always near at hand, ready to do anything I asked of him."

Do you find such comments unbelievable? In fact, as we've already seen, it's typically the mother who assumes the overinvolved role in devoted families. Usually the father's role in unbalanced devoted families is that of the emotionally distant or completely absent paternal figure.

But in some families, the dependent love dynamic takes on a different configuration. The fathers in these families, rather than being underinvolved, are in fact *over*involved with the children.

This phenomenon can take on two forms: (1) a smothering father may be coupled with an overinvolved mother to produce a team of doting parents, or (2) the overinvolved father may be paired with an underinvolved wife, for an exact reversal of the typical case that we've been exploring up to now. For families in this second category, the four parts of the Dependent Love Pattern become

- an overinvolved father, who does too much for the children and is too attached to them;
- an underinvolved mother, who is emotionally or physically distant;
- children who are overly dependent; and
- grandparents who either smothered or neglected their children.

To illustrate how these relationships may look in real-life situations, let me introduce you now to a couple of actual families, which represent each of the two smothering-father categories.

## The Co-Smothering Father

The co-smothering father is in a very subtle position. Although he smothers the child right along with the mother, he probably isn't at home most of the day with the children. Consequently, people don't notice him that much, and so he may not get blamed for spoiling the children in the same way that the mother does. Still, these nurturing, overprotective fathers may contribute just as much to the dependency of their children as the higher profile mother.

A father named John, whom I worked with in several therapy sessions, protected his daughter Dawn fiercely. John had come from a rather poor background and believed that he had had a pretty tough life. He didn't want his "little princess," as he called Dawn, to have to suffer any of the things that he had suffered. He wanted her to have the best of everything and considerable insulation from the storms and trials of life. Furthermore, no man was ever good enough for Dawn—and heaven forbid that she should ever leave home before getting married!

Unfortunately, by the time she reached age twenty-five, Dawn was not a happy princess. Instead, she had become a pampered, overprotected young lady who had no confidence in her ability to do anything on her own. In general she was miserable. As she said, she felt "torn apart," as she tried to please her parents and yet at the same time somehow become more independent and self-sufficient.

Dawn was the first in her family to come in to see me because she was so unhappy with her life. Initially she thought her problems were all her fault. But as we talked, Dawn began to understand that her difficulties arose from a family pattern that had to be corrected if she and her parents were to escape the Dependent Love Pattern imprisoning them.

One important step for Dawn was to move out of her parents' home and join some friends who had been trying to get her to stay with them. She already had a good job, and so money was no problem. Still, it was hard leaving the ever-present pampering and attention of her parents, and then trying to build a more independent life. Sure, she liked the freedom, but having to clean up her own mess and pay her own bills took some adjustments.

Before long, Dawn discovered that establishing a physical distance from her parents did help to give her a sense of independence. It was also important for Dawn and her parents to adjust their interactions. Her father had the most difficulty because his daughter had been so important to him over the years. He had devoted a tremendous amount of time and emotional energy to protecting her and, at least in his view, nurturing her development.

In fact, John had been contributing to an unhealthy dependency that prevented his daughter from achieving the very happiness and satisfaction in life that he wanted for her. Gradually, John began to understand that showing real love in this situation did not mean overinvolvement and excessive protection, but rather an affirming of Dawn's abilities and exercising less control over her.

With this realization, John was able to take some constructive steps to enable her to become more confident and independent. As difficult as it was, he tried to be more objective in evaluating her male friends when she brought them home to meet him. He and his wife also stopped acting like servants for their daughter when she visited them. They quit buying so much for her and instead encouraged her to make her own purchases. In general, they let her take control of her own life.

In other families the problems may involve a father and mother who smother their son. In one such situation, the grown son, Ron, was working for his father, Don, in the family business. They weren't getting along well, and the parents feared that they might all be heading for a disastrous rupture in their relationships.

Ron, who was still living at home, had always been his father's "prize." Don absolutely adored Ron and had given him every advantage. Having been extremely successful in his business, Don provided Ron with practically unlimited material possessions. If the son had wanted a toy when he was a preschooler, he invariably got it. If he wanted the best ten-speed bike on the market as a preadolescent, he got that. When Ron had asked for a car after getting his driver's license, Don bought him an expensive sports model.

Along with this surfeit of possessions, Don constantly bombarded his son with a steady stream of advice, corrections, and instructions. As far as both Mom and Dad were concerned, when Ron was dealing with outsiders, he could do no wrong. If he got in trouble at school, both parents would usually go in to talk to the teacher or principal. On a couple of occasions when Ron ran into problems with the police for disorderly conduct, both parents showed up at the station house with the family lawyer to back up their boy.

Somehow, it was relatively easy for Ron's parents to chalk up his teenage problems to youthful indiscretion. But then, Don invited Ron to work with him in the family business—and the young man's problems, which had been simmering for years, finally boiled over.

At first, Don didn't require Ron to live up to any particular standards on the job. Ron, true to form, didn't bother to establish any high standards of his own. As a result, he started creating problems in the workplace, with sloppy work and insensitive supervision of those under him. Before long, complaints started to pour in to Don's office, and several workers actually quit.

"What are you trying to do here?" Don finally yelled at his son. "Do you want to drive me out of business?"

Ron took the whole matter very lightly. Neither his father nor his mother seemed able to impress on him how serious the repercussions of his behavior and attitudes might eventually be.

As we discussed the family's problems, it was obvious that Ron had never been taught anything about exercising responsibility. Certainly he had been loved and cared for as much as any person could be. But both his parents had hovered over him so much, controlling his life and making things easy for him, that he had failed to learn how to resolve conflicts with other people. He lacked the simple know-how required to carry on the daily business of life. As a result, when he tried to take over responsibilities in the family business, he lacked the skills necessary to succeed.

When Ron's parents finally recognized what had been happening in their family, they seemed almost relieved to find that there were some practical steps they could take to change the situation. For that matter, Ron also brightened up at the news that his parents were going to give him more responsibility—and also help him learn some mature ways to exercise that responsibility.

It's ironic that what mothers and fathers who "co-smother" a child want most is to see their child succeed in a big way. Yet in the very act of doing everything for the youngster they make it much more difficult for the child to achieve that very success. Still, it helps when both parents have provided a strong foundation of love. With this undergirding, there's a great deal that can be done to help transform the young person's sense of being loved and accepted into a capacity to achieve and find happiness and satisfaction as a mature adult.

### The Reverse of the Classic Case: The Smothering Father and the Underinvolved Mother

Although our society often produces families with an overinvolved mother and an underinvolved father, some-times those roles are reversed. In other words, the father gets overinvolved, and the mother is underinvolved.

In one such family, Mike, a middle-aged businessman, came to me because of his deep concerns for his son Randy, who was in his early twenties. Randy had begun using alcohol and drugs. He had even been talking about killing himself.

Mike, who seemed to be a very earnest, warm, and compassionate person, said, "I really don't understand what's gone wrong here. I've tried to be available to Randy throughout his entire life. I think I do much more for him than most other fathers do for their sons. Yet he keeps having problems."

To get a better feel for the situation, I knew that I would have to meet the whole family. So we set up such a meeting for our next session.

After we had spent an hour or so together, it became clear that I was dealing with a reversal of the classic smothering-mother situation. In this family, the father was the one who had been overinvolved with all the children, including Randy. Randy, who was the youngest of three children, had experienced more difficulties in adjusting to the adult world than had his older brother or sister. His brother had completed college and was involved in an independent career, and his sister, now in modeling school, was apparently doing fine. Randy, in contrast, still lived at home and was unemployed.

The mother, Barb, had worked during her entire married life. In addition, she had attended school at night to get her college degree and then a master's in business administration. In her few free moments she had usually socialized with friends or participated in volunteer activities. Although she spoke proudly of her children, she spent little time with them. Instead, she had scheduled constant after-school and camp activities, or babysitters. When she was with the youngsters, she often was distracted by tasks she needed to get done.

Mike, in contrast, was a more naturally nurturing person. Sensing that his children might not be getting enough attention, he typically took them to school in the morning and spent several hours with them each evening. He spent a great deal of time with each youngster in activities on weekends.

Unfortunately, however, Mike hadn't emphasized the development of responsibilities and independent skills in his children. Sometimes, he would ask one of them to help out with the yard work or some other household chore. Usually, they would refuse, sometimes in disrespectful terms. All the youngsters—and especially Randy—got into the habit of "talking back" to their father. Yet Mike usually just accepted this sassiness without a word of reprimand.

Mike constantly worried about his children. He was almost always the one who would attend parent–teacher meetings at their school, intervene for them when they got into trouble with teachers, and do their homework for them. Because Barb was frequently absent in the evenings, Mike often did the cooking for the children and helped them get ready for bed.

Despite this smothering-father presence, the two oldest youngsters had managed to turn out with fairly independent attitudes—in part because the youngest child, Randy, had received an inordinate amount of his father's attention. Randy seemed to get in trouble at school more than the others, and he had more problems completing his homework assignments and adjusting in his peer relationships. Mike had, in turn, spent a great deal of his time and energy helping Randy get his life straightened out. He also had helped him out of various jams.

Interestingly, despite the attention he had received, Randy felt that he was the least favored of all the children. In part, this impression seems to have been the result of his father's attempts to help him out with his problems. With all this paternal attention, Randy got the idea that he couldn't do things for himself. He felt he was regarded as inferior to the other two children, whose achievements far outstripped his own.

In an effort to ease his frustrations and assert his individuality, Randy gravitated toward drugs, alcohol, and promiscuous sex. Predictably, these entanglements resulted in just the opposite of what Randy wanted. His father felt confirmed in his opinion that Randy was less mature than the other two children.

The picture of this family was completed when Mike described his relationship with his own parents. As the only son in the family, Mike had received excessive attention all his life from his mother. For example, she had rarely let him leave the house without checking to see if what he was wearing was just right for the weather. In her eyes, he had to be perfect in his schoolwork, manners, and appearance. Even Mike's father, unlike many other dads of his generation, spent a great deal of time counseling and guiding his son. So Mike had grown accustomed to parents who were quite attentive to their offspring, and he readily modeled his own conduct after theirs.

In an effort to redress the imbalance that had developed in this family, I recommended almost the opposite of what would normally be appropriate in devoted families with a Dependent Love Pattern. Specifically, I urged Mike to back off from his involvement in Randy's life, and I encouraged Mike's wife, Barb, to become more involved with her sons. For Barb, this meant giving up some of her outside activities and arranging specific times to spend with Randy. Also, both parents started to give Randy more responsibilities as well as more praise and support when he had positive achievements to report.

With these adjustments in the family, Randy appeared much happier and was eventually able to stop using drugs and hold a steady job. Mike and Barb, though they went through some rocky periods initially, began to spend more time together. They found ways to enjoy themselves more, now that their children were all moving on.

It's always difficult to generalize about how problems such as the Dependent Love Pattern may arise in a family because each situation has its own peculiarities and special characteristics. But as you can see, many families do fall into certain broad categories.

It's always necessary first to identify the different "players" in the family—including the dependent children, the overinvolved or distant parents, and the smothering or neglectful grandparents. Then, family members can begin to adjust their relationships so as to change a Dependent Love Pattern into more balanced loving and letting go.

In any event, whether it's the father or the mother who has become overinvolved with the child, it's clear that everyone in the family has a part in the problem, and everyone must also contribute to the solution.

# Part III

STAGES OF
DEPENDENT LOVE

# Chapter 7

# STAGES OF GROWING UP

When I used to go places with a baby in my arms and a toddler in hand, more than once an older mother told me: "Little children, little problems, big children, big problems." This piece of wisdom certainly applies to the problems of smothering concern and attention that result in the Dependent Love Pattern.

In other words, suppose you come from a devoted family in which the individuals relate in the unbalanced way that we've been describing. That is, there's an overly involved mother, probably a distant father, unusually dependent children, and either smothering or neglectful grandparents. In such a situation, you can be sure that the difficulties you may be experiencing now began very early in your life or the lives of your children.

In fact, the Dependent Love Pattern can usually be traced all the way back to infancy. At first, the consequences can be relatively small. From these early beginnings, however, the difficulties in family relationships and in individual emotional development often grow worse and become more deeply ingrained as the years pass.

Yet it's amazing how many people fail to perceive that there's a problem until much of the damage has already been done. One mother came in to see me after attending a Families Anonymous meeting, where parents describe many of the horrible situations they have faced with their children. In this particular session, a number of parents had related examples of youngsters who were serving jail terms or had been on drugs for years.

In our conversation, this mother displayed obvious feelings of relief: "I certainly don't belong in that group because my children aren't that bad. Sure, they're a little wild, but they're certainly not in trouble with the law or anything."

What she failed to see was that her children—who were only seven, nine, and twelve years of age—were entirely out of control for their age level. Probably, it would be just a matter of time, say five to ten years, before they faced some of the same problems being described by the parents of older children at Families Anonymous. In short, what begins as a small problem with young children can easily worsen over time into much more serious difficulties for older youngsters and adults.

To help you identify possible undesirable patterns with your family and children early on, I think it's helpful to take a close look at how a Dependent Love Pattern can develop over the years in a devoted family. To this end, I'd now like to lead you, step-by-step, through four major stages of dependent love, with a few practical illustrations and examples.

First, let me offer a word of caution. As we've already seen, it's extremely important to give a child lots of love throughout the growing-up process so that he will develop "roots"—a solid sense that he is loved and accepted unconditionally at home. Only with that kind of loving support can a child hope to develop the sense of competence and confidence he or she needs to function effectively in the adult world.

It's important, even as we discuss the negative effects

of a "smothering" kind of care or concern, to understand that real love should never be withdrawn from a child. One part of genuine loving is allowing and even encouraging the child to develop into an independent person. Good parenting includes the kind of love that enables the child you love to be a competent individual apart from you. When parents meddle too much or try to exercise too much control, they aren't showing genuine love at all. On the contrary, overly controlling behavior by a mother or father can contribute to a destructive Dependent Love Pattern.

In general, the smothering parental behavior that leads to this pattern may most easily be seen in parent-child interactions involving basic daily activities: sleeping, eating, dressing, and making friends. Typically, the parent who is overinvolved will try to do more for the child in these areas than the child really needs given his or her age or level of emotional development.

Now, to understand how this works, let's explore some of the helpful and unhelpful ways that parents and children may interact in each of the four major developmental stages. For each area, I'll describe the smothering approach, the other extreme of neglectful parenting, and finally the more desirable, enabling way of responding to children.

## How the Dependent
## Love Pattern Gets Started

### THE PRESCHOOL PERIOD

During the first year of life, it's virtually impossible to smother an infant with too much care and concern because at that age, every child needs a lot of loving. So you should concentrate on holding your infant, "cooing" to her, smiling at her, and talking to her (even when you know she doesn't understand completely). In general, *shower* her with care and affection!

During these first months—as well as through the first

few years of life—the child is growing emotional roots that can only come from genuine parental love. These "love roots" are absolutely critical because they provide the foundation for later confidence, self-esteem, and a sense of self-worth.

But gradually, even during this critical early stage of development, a parent should begin to encourage independence. As early as nine to twelve months, a baby begins to develop a sense that he's a separate little being. With this sense of being a distinct person comes a growing need for more inner control and autonomy. Some of the first expressions of this drive for independence occur as the child begins to crawl and walk.

*Mobility.* Parents who are caught in a Dependent Love Pattern may begin to hold on too tightly to a child when the baby is beginning to learn to crawl. For example, I knew one smothering mother who held her child almost all the time during the first year of life. She would restrain him even when the youngster was squirming to get down, flex his muscles, and roll over and scoot along the floor.

Babies are naturally curious, with a deep need to explore their surroundings. The mother who prevents this natural impulse in the name of love is really not loving her baby at all. Instead, she's demonstrating excessive control and concern and may be encouraging the development of a Dependent Love Pattern.

On the other hand, I've also seen mothers who have gone to the other extreme. One was so eager to encourage her child to become independent that she spurned his efforts to get back into her arms after he had played on the floor for a considerable length of time. It was upsetting to see the child tired and looking up into his mother's eyes with arms outstretched toward her, but with no hope of any response. Such children, far from developing a healthy independence, are more likely to become insecure, with a relatively low self-image.

In contrast, a truly encouraging, enabling, and loving

mother I know would let her growing child explore, roll, and crawl to his heart's content in a safe area. When the child tired of this brief foray into independence and exploration, she was always ready to welcome him back into her loving presence with open arms.

Similar interactions occur when a child begins to walk. The smothering parent may hover over the child, constantly saying things like, "Be careful, now! Don't fall! Watch out! Don't go too far!"

The neglectful parent, in contrast, will gratefully let the child teeter off on his own, without much regard for the sharp edges of furniture, steep stairs, or heavy objects on shelves that may pose a danger.

On the other hand, the encouraging, enabling parent will find the middle ground between these two extremes. One mother found just the right balance as she let her thirteen-month-old try out his legs. She kept an eye on him as he wandered about and periodically stumbled or fell back on his bottom. Yet every time he ran into some unusual problem, she would give him some words of encouragement, such as "Ooops! You fell down, but everybody does that when they're learning something new. Let's try again! You're really walking so well."

Many times in the first couple of years of life, the child may not understand exactly what the parent is saying to him because his vocabulary is small. Still, very young children understand much more than we think they do. They may not be able to say a particular word. But that doesn't mean they can't understand it, especially when it's delivered in a loving context, perhaps with a hug and a smile.

Concentrate on encouraging your infant or toddler with a stream of upbeat talk, punctuated by plenty of loving physical contact. As much as possible, avoid falling into a protective mode, where you play the "mother hen," shielding you're youngster from the challenges of the outside world.

In fact, the well-adjusted child should regard the world

as a series of challenges that he can overcome by himself, with only the coaching and encouragement of parents. Mom and Dad are necessary to model, teach, and provide a reassuring pat or word at the right moment to keep the child moving forward on an independent track. But independent competence—not parental protection—should always be your goal for your child.

*Sleeping.* Sleep habits in the first years of life can also play an important part in determining whether a child establishes independent or dependent behavior patterns. The main principle here is that a child must eventually learn to put himself to sleep, rather than depend on his parents to help him get to sleep. Believe it or not, sleeping properly is almost as much a learned skill as walking, eating, or socializing.

Of course, very young infants—say, up to four or five months—often don't sleep through the night simply because their digestive systems haven't developed fully and they get hungry every few hours. By late in the first year, and often much earlier, your child should be ready from a physical standpoint to sleep through the night without needing an extra input of food.

Even so, most children, including those of school age, will sometimes wake up in the middle of the night and cry out. Certainly, if the child is truly frightened or disoriented, perhaps as the result of a nightmare or illness, parents should respond and offer comfort. But I've known a number of parents who go entirely too far in responding to their children's recurrent wakefulness.

One mother and father I know would both jump out of bed and rush into their son's room at the sound of any little whimper. They would always give him a glass of juice or something to eat, and they'd either hold his hand until he fell back to sleep or take him into bed with them.

Obviously, this child, who was still locked into the same pattern of behavior when he was five years old, had nothing to lose and everything to gain by interrupting his sleep. He actually got into the habit of waking up once or twice in the middle of the night, apparently realizing he would be able to enjoy a snack and his parents' companionship. By showering their son with excessive attention, this mother and father played into a broader pattern that robbed their youngster of his ability to be independent and live his own life.

At the other extreme, another mother I know was usually quite tired when she came home from work. She felt she had no time or energy to deal with what she called the "little games" that her four-year-old daughter liked to play at bedtime. All the girl wanted was a few minutes of hugging and chatting with her mother before she drifted off to sleep. She needed a loving routine to make the transition from her active daytime life to the sometimes frightening sounds and shadowy sights in her darkened bedroom.

But the mother wouldn't have any of that! She just told her daughter, "You're too big to be afraid of silly things like the dark! Now go on to sleep!"

In this case, the daughter could definitely have used more loving attention. The mother's behavior toward her at bedtime reflected a broader pattern of neglect and inattention that expressed itself in a variety of insecurities in the child as she grew older.

A third couple chose a more enabling response to their son's bedtime needs. They established a loving routine just after the youngster crawled into bed, with plenty of hugging, kissing, reading, and chatting about the day's concerns and problems. Then, they always said a goodnight prayer and walked out of the room.

When he was very young, this boy sometimes whimpered or cried when his mother or father left the room. Usually, the departing parent would then turn around, go back to the child, pat him on the head and say, "Now, you know, it's time to get to sleep, right? I know you can get to sleep if you just lie down and relax."

Sometimes, there was some more whimpering or an

attempt to get up again. But usually, it stopped within minutes, and the child fell right to sleep. When the youngster cried for more than ten or fifteen minutes, the parents sensed that something unusual was going on. In those situations, they would go back into the room to see what was wrong. But they were firm about not accepting superficial excuses or explanations about why the youngster couldn't get to sleep. As a result, they usually found that when he continued to cry or complain, something really was wrong with him.

There is another important reason for parents to encourage their child to become independent and self-sufficient in developing his own sleep patterns. On a number of occasions, I've counseled couples whose main problem with each other was that they were both *tired*. They simply weren't getting enough sleep! In a number of situations, the reason they weren't getting enough sleep was that their children were keeping them awake. Teaching your child to sleep properly on his own will not only help foster healthy independence in him, but it will do wonders for your own health and well-being!

*Eating*. Another major area where the Dependent Love Pattern may begin to show itself in preschoolers is around the family dinner table. All parents want their children to get the right foods to eat, but smothering parents often take this concern to an extreme. I've known some parents who constantly push, prod, and complain when their children fail to eat a wide variety of foods. More often than not, though, the children actually enjoy the extra attention they're getting. The more the parent focuses on the issue, the bigger the issue becomes, and the more difficult the child is to deal with.

Some parents go so far as to continue to hand-feed a child until he's nearly school age. I recently went out to eat with a father and child at a restaurant, and the five-year-old son was strewing his food all over the table. In general, the boy didn't seem aware that his fork and spoon were more appropriate instruments for picking up food than his fingers.

The father soon explained the problem: "My wife still feeds him, so he really doesn't have any idea what he's doing over there with that food!" In fact, though, it wasn't simply Mom's fault. The entire family had become entrapped in a broader Dependent Love Pattern, where the son had almost everything done for him by his parents.

Nor do I consider myself and my own family to be immune to these smothering tendencies. I can remember when my son Joshua was about nine months old, and we had mashed potatoes for dinner.

My mother had noticed earlier that Joshua was developing a certain dexterity at the dinner table: "Did you know Joshua can eat with a spoon?" she had asked me.

I had to admit I really didn't know because I hadn't been giving him much of a chance. In fact, even after my own mom had tipped me off, I wasn't too inclined to build up his independence in this area.

I tried feeding him those mashed potatoes numerous times that evening, but he just didn't seem to like the taste of the potatoes. On the other hand, he did seem fascinated about the idea of digging into them with his spoon. I discouraged him, though, because I didn't want to have a big mess to clean up.

Finally, I gave in—and he ate the whole bowl! Of course, he had a lot of it on his face, but the joy he experienced feeding himself, and the snapshot we got of the whole scene, more than made up for the extra cleaning. Soon, his increasing ability to feed himself made a lot less work for me.

*Dressing.* At about age two, a child should be able to start dressing herself. Furthermore, she should progress steadily in this area until about age five, when she should be able to perform most of the dressing tasks an adult can do.

Of course, some of the last things to be learned include tying shoelaces, tying a tie, or pulling on a particularly tight or difficult piece of apparel, such as boots or ice skates. As long as you see progress during this preschool period, you'll know that your child is developing an important sense of control and independence—qualities that will help her avoid the traps of the Dependent Love Pattern.

On the other hand, a smothering parent may continue to dress a child beyond the time when he could actually learn to dress himself. Sometimes, parents will do a job for a child just to save the time it takes for the child to do the job himself. In other cases, the parent can't stand the idea that the child may get a little frustrated at not being able to perform a new dressing task quickly and efficiently. So the adult will step in just to keep all emotions on an even keel. Or the parent may be more concerned about how the child looks to others than about how well the child is learning to do things for himself.

This is a mistake. By intervening in this way, the parent may prevent the child from acquiring the skills and sense of assurance that he needs to develop independence. Generally speaking, if you have to make this choice, it's better to allow a youngster too much leeway in dressing himself rather than too little. A child should at least be allowed some participation in picking his daily clothing when he's as young as two or three years, By the time he's five, he should be having a major say in his outfits.

Of course, sometimes parents must put their feet down. A youngster may have to be redirected if he wants to wear torn jogging pants to a special event where all the other children are going to be wearing their best outfits. On the other hand, parents may begin to slip into smothering if they refuse to allow the child to wear slightly mismatched clothes of his own choosing. Or they may exercise too much control when they resist letting a youngster go outside in a sweater instead of a coat on a cool day.

This issue came up in my own family when I was growing up. When I would disagree with my mother's suggestion that I wear a coat, my father would jokingly bring up an old saying from his family: "Put on your coat. Your mother's cold."

Often, the reason that mothers try to control what their children wear is that they are afraid of what people outside the family will say if their youngsters don't look as good as the kids next door. Usually, however, when parents are willing to risk the disapproval of outsiders, they'll find that the attitudes of other adults are really not that fearsome.

I know one mother who was worried about the judgment of outsiders, but she eventually began to feel completely worn down by her five-year-old daughter after endless battles over what the girl would wear. Finally, on one occasion, the mother just decided to give up. She let her daughter pick out her own clothes and tried to look the other way, all the while gritting her teeth, anticipating that the child would look frightful when she emerged from the bedroom.

It's true that the daughter didn't look picture-perfect, but she certainly looked acceptable enough. In fact, she had learned some lessons well from her mother. Her skirt and blouse were color-coordinated! And when she went out to a friend's house, she was even complimented on how she had dressed herself.

An encouraging parent, then, will allow children to do as much personal dressing as possible, stepping in only when a child's feelings of frustration or failure keep him from progressing. Sometimes, a youngster will find he simply can't handle a task. But as long as a child is willing to try, the loving parent should offer encouraging advice and respond patiently, even when it takes the child three times as long to complete the job.

* * *

*Socializing.* During the preschool years, one of the most important things that children learn is how to socialize with others. If a youngster is on his own much of the time during these early years, that kind of independence can produce insecurity. On the other hand, if parents rarely give a child the opportunity to interact with his peers, such overprotectiveness can also produce insecurity.

Early on, children must learn how to get along with others of their own age. That means working through disagreements and learning to compromise or accommodate their own interests to the interests of others. Children who don't learn these interpersonal skills will often feel uncomfortable around strangers and will lack an understanding of how to make and keep friends.

One young couple resisted having their five-year-old son go to other children's houses for playdates, even though he had received numerous invitations. The parents weren't even persuaded when they learned that some of his friends regularly enjoyed the adventure of preschool slumber parties. As a result of their excessive caution, the boy missed a number of opportunities to deepen his friendships with some of his classmates in nursery school and kindergarten.

In addition, the smothering mother in this family interfered in other ways in her son's social life. At the first sign of any discord on the playground, she would step in and mediate, especially if her youngster seemed to be having a hard time dealing with the dispute. As for the boy, he came to assume that Mom would always take care of him, no matter how minor the problems that he faced on the playground or during playdates. He began to look to her rather than himself to make judgments and decisions in his peer relationships. Before long, he became excessively dependent on his mother, who was overwhelming him with her expressions of concern and care.

In addition, this mother never used babysitters, other than her own mother or mother-in-law. Many times, however, these relatives were not available, so she was left with handling almost all the child care by herself. Because the child had never learned to feel comfortable with others, he encouraged her overinvolvement by clinging to his mother when strangers were around.

Once when I scheduled an appointment to see this mother alone, she wasn't even able to keep the counseling appointment because she couldn't get her mother or mother-in-law to babysit! But as we talked, she started to see how she had gone overboard in doing everything for her son. In effect, the Dependent Love Pattern in this family was undercutting the boy's natural need to learn to become more independent.

As it happened, this woman's own mother had neglected her, and the experience had left her with many insecurities, which she was determined not to pass on to her own child. But she swung too far in the other direction. We focused most of our efforts on helping her pull back from her overinvolved relationship with her son and give him greater independence.

Gradually, she found that she could allow him to play more freely with other children without her intervention. As a result, he became more skillful at defending himself and making his own decisions in his interactions with his peers. The mother also engaged a regular babysitter—a local high school girl whom the boy soon adored—to come in every Saturday night so the parents could go out for dinner or a movie. I knew the enmeshed family was outgrowing the Dependent Love Pattern when the boy tentatively asked if he could spend the night with a friend—and the mother, to his great surprise and joy, said yes!

A major message that should come across from these preschool experiences is this: It's important to be aware that the Dependent Love Pattern can start causing trouble very early in life. Very often, the major dynamics of the Dependent Love Pattern have already been set by the time a child is ready for school. By then, it may take more work and patience on the part of the parents to break the pattern and achieve a healthier balance between love and independence with the child.

### SCHOOL-AGE SMOTHERING

The problems with the Dependent Love Pattern that begin in the preschool years are likely to continue and become even more ingrained as the child grows older. Sometimes, a problem continues during the school years in much the same form as it took during infancy or toddlerhood. For example, suppose a child can't get to sleep by himself when he's three or four years old. If the parents encourage him to be dependent on them to fall asleep, the chances are they're going to see continuing difficulties when the youngster is eight or ten years old.

On the other hand, sometimes a problem that begins in the preschool period may continue in later years, but it may be expressed in a somewhat different way. Take the challenges that a child may face in relating to her peers. If your four-year-old daughter has the benefit of your help and interruptions when she's arguing or fighting with another child, then the chances are that she may have difficulty working through other problems or making her own decisions as she gets older.

To see in more detail how some of the smothering tendencies can continue into the school years, let's begin by looking at the major categories we've already examined—sleeping, eating, dressing, and socializing.

*Sleeping.* Problems with sleep habits often don't emerge abruptly at a particular age or developmental level. Instead, they creep up on a family gradually, until one day they realize that they've let things get completely out of hand.

Certainly, you have to be realistic. Most loving parents do welcome their preschool children into their beds at one time or another. Let's face it: snuggling can be a lot of fun and a great way to start the day with a little son or daughter in the early morning hours. But when it begins at three in the morning daily, or when that cuddly three-year-old becomes a lanky, angular eight-year-old, then early morning snuggling takes on a different character.

One family with a nine-year-old boy came to me with a variety of sleeping problems, which seemed to have begun with the child, but now thoroughly involved his parents as well. First of all, the boy needed his mother to be in the room with him before he could go to sleep. He insisted that she stay right there with him until he dozed off. Sometimes, this bedding-down procedure would take a half hour, an hour, or even longer. In fact, Mom would sometimes fall asleep before her son did!

Of course, the practice interfered with her relationship with her husband, who more often than not found himself sitting in the living room alone, reading or watching television. Among other things, Mom and Dad found that they had too little time to pursue an enjoyable sex life. In the first place, there just wasn't much opportunity because the mother was spending so much time with her son in the evenings. Even when there were opportunities for sex, the mother often found that she was too tired after the hassle with her son in the evening to enjoy any physical intimacies with her husband. The husband, for his part, was often too sleepy or fed up with waiting by the time his wife finally got their son to sleep.

Unfortunately, the sleep problems didn't stop when Mom finally coaxed her son to sleep. At least two or three times a week, he would get up in the middle of the night and crawl into his parents' bed. Because he was a rather large youngster—and a wiggly one, at that—there wasn't enough room for all three of them to fit comfortably, even in the parents' queen-sized bed. As a result, Mom or Dad would actually get up and go to the boy's room or head for the living room sofa to finish out the night.

This punishing routine finally pushed their already

rocky marriage toward a crisis. The mother and father had begun to argue frequently—in part because of their lack of sleep, in part because of the frustrations arising from their son's sleeping habits.

During our discussions about this problem, we worked out a strategy by which the mother was gradually able to extricate herself from this unhealthy sleeping pattern. She realized that inadvertently she had encouraged the youngster to become too dependent on her. The father, for his part, recognized that he had stayed too removed from the situation. In some ways, he had actually helped reinforce his son's sleep problems. In any event, he had to become more involved in order to help correct the problem.

So the parents worked out some bedtime guidelines with the son, whereby the parent who was putting him to bed would spend a maximum of fifteen minutes with the go-to-sleep routine. We all felt that this was enough time to allow the parents to show their love to their son. Yet it was short enough to discourage a continuation of the old habit of seemingly endless goodnights.

The parents also laid down a rule that the child was not to come into their bedroom before 6:30 A.M.—the time when they usually got up. This way, the boy could come in for a quick snuggle just before the day started, but he wouldn't interfere with his parents' rest.

Of course, this arrangement didn't work perfectly at first. The boy sometimes came into the bedroom too early. He sometimes tested the limits set for him in the evenings, in an effort to get his mother to stay with him a little longer in his room. But both parents remained relatively firm in reinforcing the approach that they had established. Very soon, the entire family was getting a lot more rest, and the husband and wife had time together to work on improving their own relationship.

Obviously, there are other problems that may arise when a child develops inappropriate sleep habits as a result of a Dependent Love Pattern. Consider, for instance, some peculiar problems of the single mother. In addition to fatigue and the development of dependency patterns in the child, a single mother who remarries may run into her own special variety of sexual trouble. For example, her new husband will probably be even less understanding than her former husband if the child keeps his mother occupied for a good part of the evening, or tries to make himself at home in the parents' bed during the night. Such behavior is virtually guaranteed to make any new marriage more difficult from the very beginning.

As in the preschool years, sleeping is just one activity where the Dependent Love Pattern may emerge. Mealtimes may continue to be a problem area as well.

*Eating.* In some devoted families, where care and concern have gone too far, battles over eating may continue well into the school-age years. One mother agonized daily over what foods she should fix for her eight-year-old daughter's bag lunch. It seemed that no matter what she chose to pack up, the child would refuse to eat it.

Finally, the mother picked up on one of her daughter's gibes, when the girl said, "I'll bet *I* could do a better job fixing my lunches than you, Mom!"

"Okay, *you* fix your lunch from now on," the exasperated mother responded. "I won't interfere at all—just so long as you pick things that are basically healthy."

From then on, the daughter actually became enthusiastic about putting her own lunches together. In fact, she frequently started on the project the night before. True, there was less variety in her lunches than in her mothers. She seemed to have a fixation on peanut butter and carrot sticks. But at least the girl now started eating regularly, and she developed some autonomy in one important area of her life.

Parents are bound to lose if they struggle too hard with their children over food. Ultimately, you can't force any other person to eat, including your son or daughter. The children will either rebel out of resentment, or they'll go too far in complying and may encounter problems with obesity. Even more serious, eating struggles that begin in early school-age can pave the way for life-threatening eating disorders later in adolescence.

Certainly, you should have healthy foods available and encourage your child to observe basic principles of good nutrition. If you wish, you may set up certain rules that still give your child a choice, such as allowing snacks and sweets only after regular meals are eaten. Or the child might be permitted to make a choice among the vegetables being served. But no child will starve just because he turns his nose up at a few foods. So relax! Be as flexible as possible, and encourage your child to learn to make his own nutritional decisions during this critical school-age transition period.

*Dressing.* By the school-age years, children should be capable not only of dressing themselves completely, but also of picking their own clothes and even helping to shop for them. To be sure, a responsible parent should still exercise some supervision, just to ensure that the youngster doesn't make any gross errors in judgment about what clothes to wear. But all this is part of an ongoing learning process—with the final goal of independence.

In other words, even as the parent advises and directs the child about dressing during these years, the goal should ultimately be to enable the child to operate on his own, without any parental help at all. After all, adults are expected to know how to choose the right clothes, wear them in good taste, and in general, be independent with their wearing apparel. Devoted parents may feel they are caring for their children by taking care of most of their dressing needs. But in fact, they may be failing to teach them needed skills, which keeps the youngsters from growing up.

* * *

*Socializing.* One of the biggest tasks for a child during the early school-age years is to continue developing those social relationships and skills that began during the preschool period.

Specifically, the elementary school youngster should learn (1) to be comfortable when separated from parents for increasingly long periods of time, (2) to become increasingly adept at making and keeping friendships, and (3) to relate effectively to teachers and other authority figures.

Compared with children from other kinds of families, children from devoted families may find that they have relatively more trouble moving away from home and mixing with strangers for a number of reasons. For one thing, a devoted family is a great place to grow up and a very secure, compelling place to spend most of your time. Many children will prefer either to invite their friends over to their own home or just to stay there if their friends can't come over. Indeed, many children I know from such comforting families become little "homebodies" at an early age, much preferring to play alone with their toys or, if possible, to engage Mom in lengthy afternoon playdates.

To some extent, this kind of home can be a pleasing source of security in a child's life. But when love goes too far—when playing alone or just with a parent takes the place of important peer relationships—then a devoted family may be moving toward the Dependent Love Pattern.

Sometimes, for example, the attraction a child feels to his home may involve not only security and comfort, but also some subtle guilt feelings toward a parent. One mother regularly told her son how "lonely I'm going to be" when the boy was preparing to leave for a playdate. He sensed, to a great extent subconsciously, that he would be hurting his mother if he left her by herself. So he chose not to go out on these forays with friends, and consequently, his ability to make and maintain solid friendships diminished.

In this case, the mother had been unaware of the impact that her attitudes and comments were having upon her son. When she finally understood what was happening, she adjusted her relationship with him and actually began to encourage him to go out.

"I think you'll have a great time outside with Johnny," she told him. "And it would make me very happy if you'd get to know him a little better!"

This was all that her son needed to encourage him to head outdoors with his friend.

Sometimes, a dependency pattern may emerge in more subtle ways. For example, one of the most common practices among school-age children in devoted families is for youngsters first to identify a "weak spot" in the parental armor. Then, they'll begin to exploit it in some way, sometimes to the detriment of their own peer relationships.

For instance, when I was a child, my siblings and I would usually walk to school with other children. But on some chilly or snowy days—or when we were just feeling a little lazy—we'd begin to whine and beg in an effort to get my mother to drive us to school rather than make us walk. Usually, we were good enough at playing on her sympathies that we succeeded with our objective.

Granted, this is a minor sort of thing, and most children in caring families have tried this trick at one time or another. But as I remember this, I think it would have been better for me to learn that I could walk even on tough days rather than that Mother could be swayed by whining. In the long run, I doubt that my life was damaged significantly by wheedling Mom into driving us to school. But if this sort of practice goes too far—with the mother becoming the child's main companion during the formative school-age years—a destructive kind of dependence, rather than life-giving independence, may be the result.

* * *

*Household tasks.* After learning the basics of sleeping, eating, dressing, and otherwise caring for himself, a child needs to understand how to contribute to the larger household. Not only does this give him a sense of importance in having a special role in the family, but it also teaches him necessary life skills.

During this period of life, a child needs to develop a sense of responsibility and confidence that he is capable of taking on and accomplishing various necessary tasks. To this end, it's important for parents to begin to assign simple chores, such as helping to clear the table after a meal or taking out the garbage.

Smothering parents will tend to do everything for a child, even those tasks that the child can and should be doing himself. Or they may complain about not getting help, but they never teach or really expect the child to handle responsibilities. When this happens, the youngster fails to learn how to take on responsibility and doesn't become skillful and knowledgeable at helping himself and others.

In contrast, a more neglectful parent may try to force a child to do too much. For example, an older child may be given inappropriate responsibilities, such as having to care for younger siblings in ways that are beyond his capabilities. One twelve-year-old was expected to cook dinner for his brothers and sisters every evening because the mother was working. Some other parents I know made their son get to school on his own, even when it seemed dangerous to cross certain streets or negotiate certain relatively dangerous parts of town.

The enabling parent will find a middle way between these extremes. She will be sure that her son or daughter gradually takes on increasingly difficult tasks and areas of responsibility. At the same time, she'll be sure to model and teach the needed skills first. Being sensitive to the child's particular needs, she won't push him harder than he or she can manage.

It's not too helpful to say without any warning, "You're nine now. Clean up your room!" Instead, the enabling parent should start in preschool years to teach the small steps of cleaning. So, the parent might instruct, "When you take out a toy, you have to put it back before you get out another." Or, "Let me show you how to make the bed. First you pull up the sheet and fold it like this. Then, pull up the blanket. . . ." Or with cooking, the enabling parent might start with having the child help put in ingredients and stir them; then move to having him make the dish himself with some help; and finally, let him be responsible for making the dish on his own.

*Schooling.* You might think school is an area that's fairly separate from parental influence. But in fact, parents can greatly affect a child's school development. Parents can play an important role in giving their children a positive, encouraging attitude toward going to school and an ability to do their work successfully by themselves.

A parent's basic attitude toward school is conveyed very early. For example, when a child first goes to school, an overprotective mother may, either overtly or covertly, convey the message, "It's going to be hard to leave Mommy. I wonder if my baby's going to be okay without me." Such parents don't want to be like the harsh mother or father who says, "It's about time you were off on your own. Don't give me any crying or complaining!"

In contrast, truly encouraging parents, while listening to and understanding natural anxieties about doing something new, will let their child know school is an exciting new experience that he can enjoy. They won't convey this message with a hard, unsympathetic edge.

In the daily routine of sending a child to school, overprotective parents may let the youngster stay home often with minor aches and colds. When they do send the child to class, they may walk her by the hand to the classroom door.

Neglectful parents, though, may force a child to go to

school, even if the youngster is seriously ill. They may also make him go on his own, without supervision.

Unlike either of these extremes, encouraging parents will set high standards for going to school. They will let their child know the importance of school and show confidence in the youngster's ability to make it successfully through the day. These parents will encourage and praise the child for walking or riding on his own as far as he can safely and comfortably manage.

Another common area for overprotection arises when the child complains about a teacher or an event at school. An abusive or neglectful parent may not heed a child's complaints and concerns at all, even when they are valid and perhaps signal some danger.

A smothering parent will often jump in too quickly in total sympathy with the child, and consequently increase the child's dislike of school. So, if Johnny says that his teacher yells at him, his overprotective mother may want to hear about the terrors of the teacher, rather than about what Johnny was doing that caused the teacher to yell. Such a mother may go in to complain without encouraging the child to handle matters by himself. Rather than going in to hear the teacher's perspective first, this mother may talk about the teacher to the child or to friends in ways that further undermine the child's respect for the teacher.

Encouraging parents, while listening attentively to their child, will try to understand the teacher's perspective as well. Then, they will work to promote both respect for the teacher and improved behavior by the child.

Homework is another important area in which parents frequently become overinvolved. A child should be responsible for his or her own work—and that means getting it, doing it, and returning it. Teachers usually assign for homework only those things a child should be able to do himself. In fact, a principal lesson to learn from homework is how to be responsible for one's own work. A parent's job is primarily to encourage the child to do the homework and then to praise a job well done. Actual correcting or giving consequences, positive or negative, should be left to the teachers.

Many overinvolved parents may take over their children's homework, almost as if it were their own. They cajole the child into doing it and actually help or do parts completely themselves. They may keep up with school projects better than their child, and feel the pride or embarrassment of the work more intensely than their child.

The best role for a parent in such situations is to step out of the helping role and, instead, work to set basic requirements and a facilitating environment. So, a parent might help establish a quiet personal work space for a child, or help the child develop a daily plan for getting homework done. The parents might enforce a rule that no TV is allowed until homework has been completed. But daily nagging, overseeing, or doing the homework with a child isn't helpful. Such practices can easily discourage, rather than encourage personal achievement, and they should be eliminated.

Overall during the school-age years, parents need to help children to care for themselves, to take on household responsibilities, and to learn to make their own decisions. It's only through a step-by-step process of teaching children and then giving them responsibility for acting and decision-making that parents can provide their child with the best possible chance to become a mature adult.

### THE ACHES AND PAINS OF ADOLESCENCE
Up until adolescence, the child has been learning skills for independent functioning. During adolescence, however, he will have to actually perform independently in many areas. If he has not learned the skills necessary to independence, adolescence can be a truly horrible time, both for the child and for the parents.

Suppose, for example, that a child hasn't learned gradually to take on responsibilities, such as dressing himself, eating properly, and doing tasks around the home. Some parents seem to expect that because a child has reached a particular age, he should automatically know certain things, much as a duck suddenly seems to know how to swim. Such a parent may say, "You're eighteen now. You should be able to cook."

But you can't reasonably expect that child to become responsible overnight! Instead, he'll continue to act like a child whose emotional age is much younger than his age in years. My main objective in counseling with families is to help children who have been sheltered and overprotected to grow and take on responsibilities, so that their emotional and social ages will finally catch up to their chronological ages.

Unfortunately, this delayed psychological growing-up is rarely a calm, relaxed, enjoyable experience. Almost every adolescent, regardless of his emotional age, wants to be independent, even if he doesn't have the skills to take control of his own life.

There's no arguing most children out of this desire for independence. If parents don't support the healthy development of independence, their children are likely to attempt to become independent in unhealthy ways. For example, children may suddenly break away from their parents by running away or becoming pregnant. Or they may withdraw from their parents, yet demonstrate their continuing need to depend on someone or something by establishing other unhealthy, dependent relationships. Among other things, they may fall indiscriminately under the influence of immature peers and authority figures, of undisciplined sexual relationships, or of drugs.

One couple whom I counseled had two children, both of whom had remained quite dependent on their family since toddlerhood. In a variety of areas—including some of the sleeping, eating, and dressing practices that we've already discussed—the children had come to expect that their parents would do everything for them.

When adolescence arrived for the first of these youngsters, what had seemed to be a happy family unity disintegrated amid destructive behavior. The eldest child, a boy, started doing poorly in his schoolwork and began to cut classes as part of his personal declaration of independence. On one level, this boy was expressing opposition to his parents and his need for autonomy. But ironically, his actions kept him dependent on them because the mother and father became even more involved with him through his problems at school.

As the boy grew older, he started staying out late at night, dating a variety of girls, and hanging around with friends whom his parents suspected of drug use. As it turned out, the boy himself was deeply involved in drugs, as his parents realized when they discovered cocaine and various pills in his dresser drawer. When they confronted him with the evidence, he responded rebelliously, ''So what! I'm old enough—I can do what I want to!''

As independent as this boy kept trying to be, he actually became even more dependent on his parents. For example, he began to pilfer money from his parents' pockets and drawers to support his drug habit. The parents worried about him more and more and consequently, became even more involved in his life. Among other things, they spent extra time questioning him and consulting with teachers and counselors at school. There remained some amazingly infantile aspects to the parent–child relationship. Even though the boy was now eighteen years old, his mother still combed his hair for him occasionally and nagged him about what to eat. His father tried, unsuccessfully, to impose rules on him that might have been applied more appropriately to his younger sister, who was only nine years old.

Finally, the boy got his girlfriend pregnant, and his explanation was rather telling: ''Maybe my folks will realize now that I'm not a baby,'' he said. ''Maybe they'll begin treating me like an adult if they see I'm going to have my own child!''

Obviously, the problems that this boy experienced had

begun much earlier than his teenage years. Even at this point, though, it wasn't too late for him to develop a healthy independence within his family. There was still time to learn to love and be loved in a more balanced way.

At present, this boy, his sister, and his parents are trying to work through their problems and adjust their relationships. They are doing their best to eliminate the destructive Dependent Love Pattern that has created so many difficulties for them and are meeting with some success. Gradually, this adolescent is learning more about what real responsibility means, including what he must do to prepare to be a father at such an early age.

The parents, for their part, have started treating the boy more like the young adult that he is. The mother is making a conscious effort to avoid doting on him or smothering him in the little things, such as combing his hair and supervising his eating. In general, both she and her husband are making a concerted effort to treat their son as a person who is grown up and ready to assume adult responsibilities in the world.

To be sure, this family is still trying to work out a number of issues, including what the parents will do about helping to provide for their grandchild until the son gets a job. Obviously, it would be easy for their son to continue to remain dependent on them and delay his job-hunting activities indefinitely, but it appears that the parents understand the dangers of this course of action. On the whole, they seem well on the way to breaking the Dependent Love Pattern in their relationships.

Of course, this example illustrates only one way in which unhealthy dependency may wreak havoc in relationships when children reach adolescence. Other youngsters may seem to be very compliant around their parents, with little or no inclination to become independent. But underneath, they may be rebelling violently against parental authority. Often, this kind of silent inner rebellion emerges in the form of eating disorders, such as bulimia, anorexia, or obesity. Eating is one area that a parent can't control. Consciously or subconsciously, a growing number of children seem to understand that, and they are ready to act on their understanding.

With other children, the adolescent revolt in the context of a Dependent Love Pattern may occur through sex. A daughter may seem to be doing very well in school, and she may in fact be very close to her mother. But if she lacks involvement with her father, this girl may seek male companionship by acting irresponsibly in her sexual relationships with boys. Many times, girls involved in unwise sex are just seeking male attention—attention that they are missing from their fathers at home. Or they may be looking for independence from their family, and they haven't been taught any other way to achieve it.

One young woman I counseled said she had gotten married very early "just to get out of the house." As it turned out, she was from a family where the only acceptable way to leave home was to get married. Her mother, her father, and the children in the family had been caught up in a dependency pattern. This girl desperately needed to be independent, and she had learned no means of expression other than marriage.

Unfortunately, such marriages rarely work out well. They almost never produce real independence or satisfaction for the child as an adult. Instead, the dependent child tends to replay old family situations with his spouse, and the result may be an unhealthy marriage relationship or eventually divorce.

At the end of this chain of development, from infancy through adolescence to adulthood, children do finally become adults—at least chronologically. But in many ways they may still be little boys and girls emotionally, unable to separate themselves from their families or develop responsibility and coping skills as adults.

# Chapter 8

# JUST SHORT OF SUCCESS

Sometimes, a person may appear to be rather success-ful—at least on the outside. But that outer success may be seriously tainted by inner turmoil, a turmoil that arises from the influence of a Dependent Love Pattern.

Here, for example, are a few typical comments I've heard over the years in my counseling sessions:

"I just finished working on a six-month project open-ing a new branch for our company. It went great, but I didn't go out with friends during that whole six months!"

"When I finally told my friend how terrible I was feel-ing, she said, '*You* depressed? You seem to have every-thing going for you.'"

"When I called my dad to tell him about this new account I got, he said, 'That's good. But how many more do you need to really make it big in this job?'"

"I guess I should have started the master's program in my field last year. But I've been so busy watching the children for my sister and helping my parents find a new apartment that I haven't had time."

"I may be able to run our office downtown, but I'm

still sort of worried about moving to a new city and taking over the responsibility for an entirely new operation. I mean, I don't even know how to run my own home. I never even learned how to do my own laundry—I always take it over to my parents' home.''

''I know a lot of people, and I guess I'm recognized as a friendly person. But I never consult any of them about serious things in my life. If there's something really wrong, I call Mom.''

Sometimes, the adult child may be quite successful. In fact, he may even seem on the way to the top of his field. Other times, the son or daughter may achieve a fair amount, but still not rise to his or her full potential.

In every case, however, the child in a Dependent Love Pattern will, in some sense, fall short of full success. Some may not achieve what they should be able to achieve. Others will reach the heights, but deep inside, there's no real sense of satisfaction and self-esteem. Still others may never develop a really satisfying marriage or peer friendships. Overall, the outward signs of the ''short-of-success'' condition may vary a great deal. But internally, if you're a person who is suffering from this phenomenon, you are likely to experience at least one of the following feelings:

- Feel that you've never done quite well enough, or fulfilled your expectations or those of your parents.
- Yearn for your parents to say, ''Well done!''—yet feel anxious because you haven't been assured of their approval.
- Have periodic bouts of depression or anxiety, which drive you into frequent contact with your family.
- Lack contentment and experience difficulty relaxing with anything done less than perfectly.
- Feel tensions between the demands of your career or marriage and requests from your parents or brothers or sisters.

- Sense an inadequacy as you try to handle household tasks because Mom has always done the job for you.
- Encounter difficulty developing real intimacy in your peer relationships, while at the same time having your most intense relationships with your parents.

With some people, the inner turmoil that taints outer success may be expressed in eating difficulties, such as bulimia, anorexia, or a tendency to become overweight. Other people may try to escape their anxieties and frustrations by trying drugs or alcohol—often, successful but dependent adult children have plenty of money to engage in such excesses.

For those who have fallen short of their full potential, the Dependent Love Pattern may be manifested in difficulty keeping a job or completing an academic degree. On the other hand, those who do achieve in their occupations may feel they fall just short of success in their personal relationships and their emotional development. You may find that for reasons you can't even understand, you are unable to have truly intimate, secure, or fulfilling relationships with other people. This failure to find genuine intimacy with others may emerge in problematic sexual relationships.

The underlying problem is usually crippled emotional functioning. People falling just short of success are in a sense "flying," but they're not able to rise to their full height or their full speed.

How does this condition of half-success occur? What happens in families that causes sons and daughters to continue to be tied, in a debilitating way, to their parents' apron strings?

## How Half-Success Happens

Obviously, children from devoted families have a great deal going for them. In general they believe that at least one of their parents, and often both, care for them a great deal. They know that despite their faults, they are always going to be accepted by someone. They assume that they "belong"; they get the message that they're loved.

Still, even with all these positive influences, many of these children finally leave home with the idea that something is not quite right with them. Even though they may be high achievers, their successes don't quite measure up. In some respects, either outwardly or inwardly, they simply haven't been able to reach their full potential. They believe they have fallen short of complete success.

One reason for this phenomenon of "half-success" is that children from devoted families may not receive unconditional messages of love and approval. Along with the loving behavior and statements from parents, there comes a hidden message of subtle criticism. This negative communication is often a key factor in keeping a child from being fully successful or *feeling* successful, even after that child reaches adulthood. The youngster gets the impression that while he is loved and is often the focus of attention, he usually can't quite get everything right. There's always a limitation on how well he can perform a task or measure up to parental standards.

Sometimes, the criticisms from Mom and Dad may be couched with a "but." The parent may say, "I think it's wonderful that you like to read, Joan—*but* why can't you try reading something worthwhile?" Or, "You've learned a lot about kicking that soccer ball—*but* you still don't quite measure up to Johnny, so you have to keep trying harder!"

Parents may also compliment a child but then tack on a qualifier that says, "It's okay if that's the best you can do." One father I know attended a track meet at his son's school. The boy acquitted himself quite well, although he didn't win first place in anything. Commenting on a race in which the youngster had come in second, the father said, "Second place is certainly all right—if that's the best you can do. Of course, I'd like to see you come in first."

Sometimes, the criticism may be indirect, such as the parent always stepping in and doing things for a child in such a way that says, "You can't handle this job yourself." But in most cases, any subtle, underlying criticism must be fairly constant to have a negative effect on a child's personality. If a parent is communicating this sort of message regularly—and it could easily be the father, as well as the mother—the child will eventually come to believe the negative words that he's being bombarded with.

Once the assumption has been firmly implanted in a child that "I can never quite measure up," it's very difficult to uproot this idea, even in adulthood. I've counseled many men and women who have been high achievers. Yet down deep, a number of them have had the feeling that they've fallen short or that they don't deserve what they've accomplished. In the back of their minds, either consciously or subconsciously, they hear those parental criticisms echoing in everything they do: "But, but, but."

Ironically, the very act of loving a child can make that child more sensitive to these subtle criticisms. This sensitivity, in turn, makes it difficult for the child to brush off a criticism or put it into proper perspective. As a result, the child who becomes caught up in a dependency pattern may end up struggling with insecurities, uncertainties, and a general lack of confidence all his life. He may have trouble confidently and constructively handling normal criticism until he confronts the source of the problem and deals with it.

A second cause of the half-success problem is that the dependent children of devoted parents simply may not be taught the skills and techniques necessary for independent success. Why is this? Some parents just don't understand how important it is to train their youngsters in these ways. Or they may never have learned such skills themselves.

Often, children from this sort of environment are quite

intelligent, and they may very well have succeeded in their schoolwork. But problems arise when they get out from under the watchful eye of teachers and away from the supportive home environment, where everything is done for them. In an undirected atmosphere, they find that they haven't really learned to function on their own.

What these adult children need to achieve full success in their lives is simply some training in the practical "how-to's" of achievement. For example, in areas such as keeping their room clean or making friends, children may not have been taught, step-by-step, how to do for themselves. When they encounter adult responsibilities later—such as finding an apartment, developing a budget, or traveling alone, they may have to learn the necessary skills completely on their own.

Of course, adults in these situations *can* manage to learn and do a great deal, but they could learn more quickly and achieve greater success if they had been taught similar skills when they were younger. If you are a parent, don't think this means that you have to become an instant expert on everything. It's not really essential for you to know exactly how to do something that your child is trying to learn. If you just teach the child *how* to learn (e.g., by reading books, or finding and asking people who know), then he or she will be placed in a stronger position to achieve successes throughout life.

Adult children may also need this kind of practical instruction as they try to make up for a failure to develop skills and a sense of competence when they were younger. For example, they may have to learn the basics of formulating a budget, hosting a dinner party, or meeting new people by studying a how-to book, taking a practical course, or consulting a knowledgeable friend. In any case, whether the child is young or old, as he is developing these skills, he needs some explicit encouragement: "You *can* do it if you'll just take a little time to learn *how* to do it!"

Another related problem involves the demands placed

by the family on an adult child who has become successful in worldly ways. Often, this man or woman is expected to share talents and abilities with those at home. After all, the parents have done a great deal for their children, so why shouldn't the children be expected to do just as much for their parents, sisters, and brothers?

Certainly, loyalty and generosity can be strong, positive traits in devoted families. But if these qualities are overdone, they can become burdensome and even crippling. At what point does one's responsibility to and involvement with the family become disabling, rather than supportive?

One test is to ask whether a child is being pressured to do something for another person which that person should be able to do for himself. In fact, if the child is doing more than necessary for a parent or sibling, the helping child may actually be smothering or crippling that person.

So, a son whose parents have come from Cuba may become an English translator for his parents for a far longer period of time than is necessary or desirable. Or an older sister may be asked to get a younger sister a job rather than have that younger sister learn the skills of job-hunting and experience the rewards of self-confidence for herself.

Of course, there are some seeming benefits, such as enforced closeness, that may arise from continuing requests that a family makes of an adult child. But when family members fail to learn independent skills, they may remain dependent on each other indefinitely. Such artificial closeness is a far cry from the voluntary generosity or free enjoyment of one another that characterizes healthy, loving families.

## Some Short-of Success Stories

Half-success comes in many types, shades, and variations. Let me introduce you to three not-fully-successful adult children—Margo, Carla, and Charles.

* * *

*Margo, the international executive.* In many ways, Margo represented the dream of the modern American woman. Although only in her late thirties, she had risen far in the world of international finance and business. As a senior vice president in a major international manufacturing firm, she had been working for the last four years in Paris. Margo's high six-figure income went a long way in helping her enjoy the sights of Europe and maintain an enjoyable social life.

She had been involved in love affairs with two well-known men, though unfortunately, from her point of view, there had been no future with the relationships because both were married. Still, she had become the envy of her old school classmates in the United States, who had kept in touch with her.

But that was just the outside, the veneer of Margo's life. What was going on inside was not quite so compelling or attractive.

For the last couple of years, Margo had been suffering from severe headaches, ulcers, and an ongoing sense of depression. She had sought help from a variety of medical doctors, both in Europe and in the United States, who found no major physical problems. Gradually, the real emotional source of her problems began to emerge. It seems that even though Margo was far away from her American home, she still felt the grip that her family had on her, including tremendous conflicts that she had developed over the years with her mother.

After trying unsuccessfully for years to please her mother, Margo had given up and had gone to great lengths to sever ties with her family. She had cut off regular contact and had moved thousands of miles away and established a residence and a new set of friends in a foreign country—but this hadn't been enough. She still felt the strong tug from her family roots.

Margo had always had an intense relationship with her

mother, Jane. The mother had doted on her daughter, who was her only child and who was extremely intelligent and beautiful. Jane had gained much pleasure from her girl's accomplishments.

As a consequence of this close relationship, Margo had always wanted to live up to her mother's expectations of her, yet she could never quite reach Jane's standard. One of the problems was that her mother frequently criticized, prodded, and nagged her to excel and rise to greater heights in her achievements—even though Margo might in fact be accomplishing much more than her peers. Margo could be at the top of her class or in first place in a contest, yet her mother would still demand more.

A classic example of this attitude occurred when Margo had won an all-city mathematics prize and almost simultaneously had been elected to a high student government office. "You did real well, Margo, and I'm proud of you," Mom said—and she should have left it at that. But she went on: "You know, though, there's always room for improvement. I think if you had tried just a little harder you might have won the city prizes in Latin and literature as well."

Margo's mother also tried to exercise an exacting control over Margo's time and affection. If any activities or people threatened to take Margo away from her, she would fiercely criticize them or Margo.

Margo's father, an attractive and intelligent man, was too preoccupied with his own career to give Margo's accomplishments much recognition. As a well-regarded surgeon in Boston, he was absorbed with furthering his practice and enjoying the benefits of his work. Margo's mother had always resented his absence and lack of attention to her and their marriage. With Margo's arrival, Jane had compensated for this lack by throwing herself into the relationship with her daughter.

As Margo grew older, her achievements in her college

academic work and later in business increased—but so did the criticism that she received from Mom. Margo felt compelled to touch base with her mother several times a week, even when she was living abroad. But instead of constructive words of wisdom, what she would usually hear would be a litany that went something like this: "It's time you got married! . . . I can't believe you're involved with a married man! . . . You've been overseas long enough—why don't you see if you can't arrange a transfer back to the States? . . . If that last picture you sent me is any indication, you're not taking very good care of yourself over there! . . . Don't you ever go to the hairdresser?"

It would have been tempting for an outsider looking at this situation just to say, "Margo should cut her ties with her mother and live her own life!"

But it wasn't that easy. Because she was trapped in a Dependent Love Pattern, Margo desperately needed to maintain her emotional ties with her mother. Somehow, she had to find the approval from both Mom and Dad that she had never been able to achieve. As it was, she was setting herself up to fall short of true success in several ways: by continuing to seek the ever-elusive approval from her mother and father; by getting involved in unsatisfying, nonaffirming relationships, such as those with married men; and by moving into other dead-end situations in her personal and professional life. Even if she had received another promotion or two, she wouldn't have been able to enjoy her achievements.

As we can see from Margo's example, whether a person is across the world or across the street, physical distance cannot resolve the problems of emotional overinvolvement with parents. In fact, the tensions, conflicts, and dependence in those family relationships can intensify as the distance increases because there's little opportunity to engage in real, life-changing communication, or to take steps to heal those relationships.

In the natural course of her career development, Margo

was transferred back to the States, to a city near her parents' home. Fortunately, she recognized that it was important for her to maintain her life fairly independently of them. At the same time, she realized she needed to work with her parents to change the unbalanced relationships. To help her do this, Margo began family-oriented therapy sessions. Through these sessions, Margo was able to see the destructive patterns in her life. She learned new approaches to both family and peer relationships—approaches that enabled her finally to enjoy her success.

Periodically, her parents joined her for a session; they realized that if they wanted to see and enjoy their daughter, they would have to help resolve the tensions. Together, the three of them started dealing with some of the deep-rooted dependency links that had fostered the problems. Specifically, Jane learned to recognize her own emotional needs and find ways of meeting them besides holding on so tightly to Margo. When she was told clearly about the negative impact that her subtle and not-so-subtle criticisms were having on Margo's self-confidence, she was actually somewhat surprised. She had thought she was being helpful in watching out for her daughter.

Margo's father was only vaguely aware of his excessive preoccupation with his career, which had kept him too emotionally distant from his wife and daughter. Whenever he had experienced any fleeting guilt feelings about his lack of involvement with his family, he had just pushed those feelings aside. In our sessions he came to realize the critical impact he was having, and he proved willing to work to save his family.

This family is now in the process of adjusting their relationships so that the mother is becoming less involved in her daughter's life. The father is becoming more involved, not only with his daughter, but also with his neglected wife. These changes by the parents have freed Margo to express her talent without paying the high physical price of headaches, ulcers, and depression.

There are no quick and easy solutions in a situation

like this. After all, in Margo's case, the problem had taken nearly four decades to develop. The family couldn't expect everything to be completely corrected in a matter of days, weeks, or even months. But like many devoted families, the parents here were deeply concerned about the welfare of their daughter. They were also intelligent and sensitive enough to understand that *all* the family members had to pull together to help correct the situation. As a result, Margo is gradually moving to a point where she may be able to enjoy the all-around success in life that she so fervently desires.

*Carla, the caring professional.* Carla, a twenty-eight-year-old nursing specialist, had always been a model of the conscientious daughter and worker. Her parents had immigrated to the United States from Italy when Carla was just a toddler, and the family had little in terms of the material things of life. But through intelligence and hard work, Carla's father, Michael, managed to build a highly successful grocery business in a large city in the Northeast.

Unlike many other fathers who have devoted so much time to their work, Michael became deeply involved in the lives of this three children, of whom Carla was the eldest. He spent a great deal of time with them while he was at home, and he emphasized that if they would just work hard enough and take advantage of their opportunities, they too could be assured of success in America.

Carla's mother, Maria, was equally concerned and involved with her children's development and success. She constantly advised them and often criticized them when she felt they were getting off the straight track to personal achievement. But even as Maria and Michael participated so heavily in their children's lives, they did so with a loving hand. They may have prodded and even pushed— but at the same time, they always made it clear that they had each youngster's welfare and future at the forefront of their minds.

Both parents came out of devoted families themselves, where their parents, and especially their mothers, showed them a great deal of attention, care, and concern. Maria and Michael also learned that children must learn to do for themselves and for others in the family. They must not be just the recipients of help and service from others. As a result, Maria and Michael taught Carla and their other children that it was important for the youngsters to care for each other and to help out with family chores and responsibilities.

Carla understood from an early age that she was loved and accepted unconditionally by her parents, even as they encouraged and pushed her to achieve and excel. She grew up with the understanding that she had to look out for her younger brothers whenever they were in need of help. Furthermore, she was expected to pitch in and help her parents whenever they asked for her assistance. Refusing to help when you were asked was totally unacceptable behavior in this family.

Unfortunately, Carla, as the eldest, bore the brunt of the family's teaching and instruction about obligations and duties to others. As a result, she found she had the weight of responsibility for taking care of her brothers. As she grew older, she had to share many of the burdens that had previously been borne by her busy parents. She frequently had to help out with the cooking and cleaning around the home. In addition, she was usually the one designated to take her younger brothers to sports events and other activities when her parents were not available.

Despite these many obligations and duties, Carla was by nature a high-energy, upbeat person able to shoulder many tasks and perform them all quite well. She managed to get through college and graduate school with a good academic record, even as she maintained her various family ties and responsibilities. In fact, it didn't become evident that she really had any particular problems until she herself finally received a promotion to a supervisor's position and then met Ron, a young business executive.

By any definition, Ron was a hard-charger in the business world. He had big ambitions, which included rising to the top of his company in record time, and these objectives didn't leave much room for sticky family ties or emotional problems. As he and Carla became more serious about their relationship and began to discuss marriage, they agreed that they would wait several years to have children. That way, they could minimize any family entanglements that might get in the way of their careers. They also understood it was important for both of them to do well in their careers and establish a wise investment policy so that they could achieve financial security at an early age. When they first surveyed their prospects for the future, everything seemed in order. But Ron didn't anticipate what he would encounter with Carla's family.

After they became engaged, Ron discovered that Carla felt an obligation to drop by her family's home almost every evening before she finally went to her own apartment. Carla spent many hours each week advising her younger brothers, now twenty-two and twenty-six, or doing errands for them. She seemed to spend an inordinate amount of time every evening on the phone with her mother and father, chewing over the details of each family member's life. Whenever anyone in the family had a difference with anyone else, it seemed that he would call Carla.

To Ron, coming from an independent-minded midwestern background, Carla's involvement with her family seemed ridiculous and immature. He began to resent not only the time but also the constant concern Carla focused on her family.

The last straw came when Carla broke down in tears one evening as she related the news that her superiors in her hospital had warned her that if she wasn't willing to be more flexible about her working hours and put in more time on the job, she might not be promoted any further.

"It's no wonder you're having trouble at work," Ron said. "Look at how much time you spend focusing on your family! If you paid more attention to yourself and your career and our relationship—and less to your parents and brothers—I think you'd find that a lot of your problems would disappear!"

As you might expect, this bit of advice was not well received by Carla. She and Ron proceeded to have one of their worst arguments, and she eventually threatened to break off their engagement. Finally, after a calmer discussion the next day, Carla realized that before she got married, she needed to take some serious steps to adjust her relationship with her family. Before long, she was sitting opposite me in my office, and we began to explore some of the family interactions that had pushed her into the situation where she now found herself.

Carla explained the feelings of being pulled by her family in one direction and by her career and personal life in the other. As she put it to me one day, "Sometimes, I get the feeling that I'm going to be pulled completely apart, split right down the middle, because I just can't choose between my own life and my parents."

In fact, as I told her, it's not simply a matter of choosing between her parents and her career or personal interests. Rather, the key is to *adjust* the relationships toward a healthier adult balance. She had learned to put such a priority on family that it was jeopardizing her ability to succeed as an adult in her work and relationships.

The problems Carla faced were not easy to resolve. The love in her family was so strong that she had great difficulty pulling back from her overinvolved relationship with her mom and dad. It was impossible for her to turn her back on the strong sense of responsibility and obligation that she had developed over the decades toward her brothers and her parents.

Gradually, bit by bit, she began to give up some of the helping roles that she had been fulfilling for her parents and her brothers. She realized that what she had been doing wasn't helpful for them or her. At the same time, she started paying more attention to her adult responsibilities, including those involving her career, her boyfriend, and herself.

It was especially hard for Carla because she really was dealing with both a mother and a father who cared about her so much that they became overinvolved with her life. Through very subtle interactions in their relationships, Carla had come to believe that the very real love she experienced at home had imposed on her an obligation to return that love solely in the terms that had been defined by the family rules she grew up with. Her challenge was to establish her own new rules as an adult . . . rules which included family loyalty and responsibility, but did not jeopardize her top priority—current relationships—and her responsibilities as a mature adult.

*Charles, the artistic prodigy.* Roberta, a mother and housewife in her fifties, walked into my office in a state of shock. She had just learned that her son, Charles, a boy she described as "the pride of my life," was homosexual.

Roberta had invested a great deal of herself—of her time, energy, and maternal emotions—in Charles, and it had always been very important for her that he succeed. An older son had run into a variety of emotional, academic, and career problems, and Roberta sensed that Charles was her "last chance to succeed as a mother." But now, at age twenty-five, with a string of successes already behind him as a professional pianist and singer, Charles had walked through the door and said, "Mom, I'm gay."

This was a bitter pill for Roberta to swallow. For one thing, success by her definition didn't encompass homosexuality. She was a devout Catholic and agreed wholeheartedly with the church's position that active homosexuality was a sin. Moreover, she was well aware of the risks to her son's life from AIDS. So Charles's news came as quite a blow to her.

When she first came to me, Roberta's husband, Tom, didn't know about Charles's secret. Furthermore, because Tom had always remained emotionally distant from all the family members, Roberta expected that she could keep him in the dark indefinitely. Still, Roberta felt that Charles's involvement in homosexuality was a clear signal that she really needed to seek some sort of professional help to deal with the disturbing family developments.

As we talked, it became evident that Roberta had been, in many ways, a classic smothering mother. With such an introverted and uncommunicative husband, she had given free rein to her naturally outspoken, extroverted, and opinionated nature. At every opportunity, she had tried to dominate her family life, including the careers and personal interests of her sons. Obviously, things had not gone quite the way she anticipated. Charles, though extremely successful at work, was wrestling with a number of personal identity problems. He had headed in a sexual direction that Roberta abhorred.

As Roberta told it, she and Charles had been in an extremely close relationship since he had been an infant. "He was the cutest, most adorable little baby you've ever seen!" she said.

In may ways, she had tried to keep him almost in a state of emotional suspended animation, apparently in a vain effort to preserve his infantile cuteness, even as he grew older. Her husband, Tom, was a military man, and a strong disciplinarian at home. But otherwise, he left the daily management of the home and the bulk of child care to his wife. He made no effort to participate in Charles's academic or extracurricular development. As a result, he remained extremely distant from Charles throughout his childhood. It was natural that mother and son would move into a closer and closer bond with one another.

While Tom was in many ways a silent and distant father and husband, when he did communicate, he usually argued or made hostile comments about the way his wife was running the house or bringing up the children. In addition, Charles, despite his excellent academic performance throughout his school years, never quite lived up to his father's expectations. Tom made it clear that the only thing he really respected was "being squared away" or "showing you're tough," in the military terms to which he was accustomed. Charles, being a delicate boy who was small for his age, certainly didn't live up to those requirements. Predictably, Tom never made any effort to help Charles develop into a better athlete.

Charles retreated further into his relationship with his mother. Many times, he found himself thrust into the role of consoling and comforting his mother after she had engaged in an upsetting and sometimes violent fight with her husband. At other times, he might sit for hours on end while she confided various personal concerns to him.

As we moved further into the counseling sessions, I discovered that there were definite limits on what could be done in repairing and adjusting the injured relationships in this family. Tom was reluctant to come in for sessions, and even when he agreed to attend, he frequently backed out at the last minute or arrived late. Charles also balked at counseling because he had firmly established a new way of life in the gay culture. In some ways, he found this experience to be a relief from the conflict and overprotectiveness he had encountered in his own family. But eventually, he did agree to participate.

One of the main things that motivated Charles to become involved in the therapy sessions was that he realized something was wrong with him emotionally, even though he was doing quite well as a musician. He had always assumed that if he could be chosen for certain performances or honors, he would be happy. Having achieved a number of his ambitions at a very early age, though, he discovered he wasn't happy at all.

He continued to have problems in the homosexual relationships that he tried to establish. Among other things, he found that he usually became involved with homosexual men who were dominant and controlling, much as his own mother had been. He did not freely express his own independent opinions or interests.

Charles began to realize he had never really explored and developed a comfortable adult identity of his own. He acknowledged that he didn't get along well at all with his mother, father, or brother when he went home for visits. In fact, things at home seemed to be getting worse.

In our counseling, we focused on building basic communications skills between the family members and on correcting the imbalances in closeness and distance in the family relationships. Tom frequently indicated that he was ready to pull out of the counseling sessions. But because he realized that he was critical to any possible relief for his wife and son, he resolved to stick it out. As for Charles, he seemed to be learning more about how his family relationships contributed to the lack of fulfillment in his personal and sexual life. Most important of all, he developed an understanding and even some affection for his father, whom he had never really gotten to know during childhood.

It often takes a great deal of thought and effort to identify problems and sort out the emotional threads and themes that need to be changed, but it's important to understand that things *can* be changed for the better. It's not necessary to take a fatalistic attitude toward any behavior, even behavior of adult children. As an adult, you can make changes in your actions and reactions with family members—changes that will help you alter destructive patterns. If you can get several family members working together to resolve a problem, the effort will go a long way to heal hurts, turn smothering concern into real love, and enable children to savor and enjoy to the fullest their achievements in life.

You may feel that you have fallen just short of success in your career or personal relationships. But it's not necessary to remain there. With some genuine effort and understanding, you can move ahead and transform half-success into total success and true satisfaction.

## Chapter 9

# WHEN MOM (OR DAD) MAKES IT A THREE-WAY MARRIAGE

The interfering mother-in-law has been the target of many jokes and searing comic scenes. Even the Scottish anthropologist, Sir James George Frazer, though not intending to be facetious, may have contributed to the biting humor surrounding the spouse's mom when he wrote in his classic 1890 work, *The Golden Bough*: "The awe and dread with which the untutored savage contemplates his mother-in-law are amongst the most familiar facts of anthropology."

Do mothers-in-law really deserve all this derision and bad press? Do they have an innate inclination to show up where they're not needed or speak up at the wrong times? Do they typically dispense destructive advice and comments that may interfere with or even debilitate or destroy the marriages of their children?

In fact, I've discovered in my counseling that the "interfering mother-in-law" is usually simply a symptom of a larger family pattern—the Dependent Love Pattern. Although she is the one who is often blamed or held up as the scapegoat, everyone else in the family contributes to the tension and hostility. Her overinvolvement, along with her husband's underinvolvement, has been going on for years, and the child's marriage just serves as the current spotlight for the problem.

I'm reminded of one young woman who got married and then insisted that she and her husband live in the same apartment building as her parents. Her husband went along, and for the first few years of their marriage, the young couple and the in-laws got along fairly well. The daughter, in particular, was quite satisfied because she was able to continue her extremely close relationship with her mother. The husband didn't complain greatly since this arrangement left him free to go out frequently with "the boys."

Then the daughter and her husband had a child, and their home was no longer big enough to accommodate them. At the husband's insistence, they bought a new house only about a half hour away from her parents. Although they were still relatively nearby, the daughter began to feel deserted and very much alone. Both mother and child had difficulty making friends. This was a skill they'd never needed before. And the husband, who was used to simply providing financially, was resentful of his wife's sudden pleas for help at home and more emotional support.

Another couple had managed to make it through nearly ten years of marriage, and they had fulfilled responsibilities at work, home, and church. But periodically, they would get into big arguments. When this happened, the wife would often say, "Well, I guess it's time for me to take a vacation for awhile."

Her "vacation" was always to go to her parents' home, several hours' drive away in the next state. There, she would spend several days—or even several months during the summer—with Mom and Dad. Although these trips appeared simply to be normal family visits to outside observers, they really amounted to emotional "time outs" for the woman and her husband to cool off.

In this case, both her mother and her father welcomed her. Neither encouraged her to try to stay at home and work out her problems with her husband. As they said, they loved to see her and the grandchildren as much as possible. It wasn't until she came in for counseling due to severe headaches that this woman realized there was considerable unresolved tension in her marriage. One of the first things she had to do was to learn to work out the conflicts with her husband, rather than run away to her parents.

In short, this young wife, and even her husband, had begun to rely on her parents as an escape valve. They had failed to understand that they needed to work out their differences. When they finally accepted the fact that escape was no answer, they began to learn to argue constructively and develop a more intimate and satisfying marriage.

There are many ways that a three-way marriage may emerge. But in every case, the ultimate solution is for the couple to work hard to develop a *two*-way or *two*-party marriage. The goal is a relationship in which the husband and wife act together, without outside family interference, to resolve their difficulties and develop intimacy.

## The Basic Principles for a Two-Party Marriage: You Must "Leave" and "Cleave"

In all my reading in the psychological and marriage therapy literature, I've never encountered a better approach for creating a good marriage than this passage from Genesis: "Therefore shall a man leave his father and his mother, and shall cleave unto his wife: and they shall be one flesh" (Gen. 2:24). The basic principle of "leaving" and "cleaving" in this passage is exactly what's needed to break a Dependent Love Pattern that is reflected in marital tensions.

In this ordering of family relationships, the Bible points out that it's first necessary to *leave* one's father and mother, in the sense of striking out on your own to lead an independent adult life. Then, you *cleave*, or join strongly with your marriage partner.

In my marriage seminars, I always begin with the importance of leaving the family of your childhood as you attempt to build a healthy marriage.

### WHAT "LEAVING" IS—AND WHAT IT'S NOT

The most obvious meaning of "leaving" is physically moving out of your parents' home. This is a good starting place for considering whether you have really "left" your parents. Or, if you're a parent, it's a good point to start in seeing whether or not your children have really left home.

Don't be fooled into thinking that physically "pulling out" is all there is to "leaving." After all, most married couples don't live with their parents, but many still have not fully "left" Mom and Dad. To illustrate these points, let's consider a few classic variations on the "leaving" scenario.

*The broader meaning of "moving out."* Leaving, first of all, means becoming physically independent, rather than dependent upon, your parents. Being physically independent includes not only moving out to a separate apartment or home, but also moving out in other physical ways, such as paying your own bills, and doing your own cooking and cleaning.

Consider two typical adult children, who illustrate completely different meanings of "moving out." One has moved out of his parents' home physically, but he's still living nearby in a house owned and maintained by his parents. He usually checks in with a visit or call whenever he comes or goes from his place. His mother does most of his cooking and cleaning for him.

The other adult child is still living in her parents'

home, but she stays in a separate apartment upstairs and pays them market rent. She comes and goes as she pleases, without checking in with them. She takes complete responsibility for herself and her family in terms of cooking, cleaning, shopping, and other household responsibilities.

Which child comes closer to having "left" the parents physically? Obviously, the answer is the second one because even though she is closer in physical proximity, she is less dependent in her overall lifestyle.

Many parents and children may object that it costs a great deal for young people to make ends meet these days—so really, what's wrong with the parents' helping out a little? I find, however, that many parents don't realize the emotional cost that is exacted by having a child remain dependent on Mom and Dad. The child "pays" in terms of not feeling competent, not being his or her own person, and not being encouraged to develop personal talents and skills.

Even if a child must live at a lower standard than that to which he has become accustomed with his parents, the independence he enjoys will help give him a sense of his ability to function as an adult in the real world. Certainly, very few people in their early twenties can afford to live as well as their parents do at forty or fifty. But the experience of "making it" for yourself is more important than the extra luxuries that the parents might be able to provide. In fact, the best way a parent can care for an adult child is to enable that child to care for himself.

*The dangers of excessive contact with Mom and Dad.* Leaving your parents generally means fewer contacts with them, but the idea of cutting down on parent–child interactions can be profoundly disturbing to those from devoted families.

That telephone commercial that says, "Reach out and touch someone," strikes a responsive chord in many who come from close, caring families. After all, dutiful sons and daughters are supposed to keep in touch regularly with Mom and Dad—aren't they?

Often, those in devoted families assume that the more contact between child and parents, the better, even after the children have gotten married. Yet, in such situations, too much parent–child contact can actually cripple a marriage.

Think, for a moment, about how normal emotional growth takes place in a child. A toddler spends less time in his mother's arms than an infant does. A healthy adolescent will spend less time with parents than an elementary school child. The reason: the child's needs to be with his parents become less urgent as he learns to take care of himself.

By the same token, a mature adult child should not need his parents to care for him. Certainly, family ties may remain strong, and the parent–child relationship should always be unique and special. But ideally, a parent–child relationship should eventually be a mutual adult tie, based on love and common interests, not on dependence.

Yet some dependent adult children may carry on excessive contact with parents, with a resulting destructive overattachment to Mom or Dad. One young wife would stop by her parents' house nearly every time she went out. She'd call her mother for advice on everything from shopping, to cooking, to cleaning, to the minute details of rearing her two-year-old son. After keeping track of her activities for a week at my suggestion, she found she was averaging five contacts a day with her mother!

Another middle-aged married woman's mother had come to depend on her daughter for physical help after a minor stroke. The mother also felt she needed special comforting to make up for all the trouble she had experienced from her alcoholic husband and sons.

It turned out that the daughter fell into the habit of calling her mother ten to fifteen times a day! Understandably, her husband sensed the low level of importance he held in his wife's life and he failed to take on much responsibility around the house. In fact, after coming home each evening for a quick shower, he'd usually go out to get a bite to eat and then find some way outside the home to entertain himself.

Another adult son was accustomed to telling his mother everything about his life, including rather personal details. Even though he had finally married at age thirty-five, he continued to speak with her at least once a day. He left all his money in joint accounts with his parents, and he consulted them frequently about the details of his finances, as well as about his work problems. In fact, his mother knew more about his daily life than his wife did.

*How should you keep in touch?* As you consider the frequency of your contacts with your parents, it's important to recognize that each family is a little different from the next. There are also cultural differences from family to family. For example, for adult children from some cultures, calling parents once a week may seem neglectful. On the other hand, children from other cultures may feel that once a week contact reflects too much attachment. One of the first steps toward keeping in touch in a healthy way is to see what seems appropriate, given your particular family background.

Next, think about whether your contact with your parents is more than what your husband or wife feels is appropriate. Are you calling up to ask about things that you could reasonably do for yourself? Or are you still taking on a counseling or consoling role for Mom, which Dad or a friend of your mother's should really be doing? If the answer to these questions is yes, you're probably too involved in parental contact.

Suppose, then, you determine that you are playing too much of a dependent, childlike role with your parents. To adjust the situation, you might reduce your contacts with Mom or Dad by depending more on your spouse or peers than on your parents for help and advice. You can also encourage your parents to turn more to each other and to their peers.

In addition to reducing your contact with your parents, it's just as important to change the *kind* of contact you have with them. In this regard you might ask yourself a few key questions: What particular role do you play with the parent or parents with whom you feel you are having inappropriate contact? Write down exactly how you interact, including the way you're dependent on one another. What role do you think you should be playing with your parents? How can you begin to make a switch in roles in your very next contact with Mom or Dad?

For example, you may still be playing the role of "needy child" by calling to discuss your frustrations of the day, or to get some piece of advice that you could easily get elsewhere. Instead, try turning to your mate or friends to fulfill those needs. If you usually call Mom to ask how to cook things, learn how to put together a new dish without her help. Then, call Mom to share your success at cooking on your own. In these ways, your mother will start to see you as a more capable adult.

As we've seen, some adult children also play the role of counselor to their parents, even though they have little time or emotional energy for this responsibility. If this describes you, turn the tables on them. Try turning to them for advice or support for your own needs!

If your mother calls to complain about your father or to ask your support in dealing with one of your siblings, tell her you know she can handle the problem because she's had much more experience than you have. Then, direct the conversation to some of your own needs and goals so that you can get out of the counselor role with her.

I realize, of course, that it's often not easy to shift conversational patterns and underlying relationships because they often reflect interactions that have been going on for years. Still, making small adjustments over a period of weeks and months can go a long way toward achieving a better balance in family relationships. Even as you lessen or change your contacts with your parents, remember that it's important to continue to show your love for them and let them know how much you appreciate them.

Up to this point, we've focused our "leaving and cleaving" discussion mostly on your relationship with your parents. But what about your spouse? Obviously, it's important always to evaluate your interactions with your parents in light of those with your spouse. One helpful way to keep things in proper perspective is to take a close look at the priorities in your life.

*What has first priority in your life?* A very important way of testing whether or not you're "leaving and cleaving" properly is to ask yourself, "Who gets the first priority or allegiance in my life?" When you must choose between a parent and your spouse, whom do you usually pick?

The issue may be as simple as whom you choose to talk to on a given occasion. Suppose, for example, you've had a long, difficult work week, with no opportunity to sit down and get up-to-date on activities and feelings with your spouse. Do you actually sit down for a long extended talk with him or her? Or do you choose instead to discuss your problems in an extended phone call with one of your parents?

There are many other ways to test your priorities. For one thing, you might consider your motives for decorating and maintaining your house: Are you primarily interested in pleasing your parents, or your spouse? When there's an argument or disagreement involving your parents and your spouse, whose side do you usually take?

Many times, you may not have to choose between your parents and your husband or wife. But if you're like most people I know, there are frequently times when you do have to make some subtle choice. The direction you select will indicate who gets first place in your life. Everyone has a primary attachment in life with some other person. If you remain mostly attached to Mom or Dad, that tie will prevent you from successfully joining with a partner in a healthy and productive marriage union.

*How to "leave" the emotional hold of an absent parent.* When a parent has died, lives far away, or is otherwise absent, some children may idealize that parent or try to live up to imagined parental standards of perfection. Yet such an attitude can cause even an adult child to feel as though he or she always falls short of true success.

Other children may harbor hatred, subconscious hostility, or unresolved conflicts with a parent. Like the idealization of a parent or the attempt to conform to parental ideas of perfection, these negative feelings may prevent the child from moving on to become an adult responsible for his or her own behavior.

One young woman, whose father died when she was only eleven years old, has had tremendous difficulty developing productive, positive relationships with the men in her life. Her dad was a very warm, supportive person, and during the years that she knew him, she came to adore him as the perfect male figure. At the same time, however, her father had incredibly high standards for his children. Consequently, she never felt that she had quite been able to live up to them.

Because this young woman constantly carried these strong feelings, she found that for years she regularly became involved in relationships with men who fell short of her expectations. She always hoped that her male friends would take care of her and nurture her, much as a father would nurture a daughter. But her men always disappointed.

Furthermore, she found that many times both men and women failed to treat her with respect, apparently because she projected an image of being very dependent on others. She whined, wheedled, and sometimes even begged people to do things for her. Such efforts usually backfired. In fact, this woman has been married twice, and her current husband has been threatening to walk out on her. He frequently becomes frustrated with her because he feels that she expects too much from him and is never pleased with him.

In working with this woman, I've had to focus on adjusting her relationship with her dead father. Among other things, we've explored ways in which she may have idealized him to the point that he has become a fantasy figure.

For, in actuality, the facts show that Dad wasn't exactly perfect. We've learned from her mother and older brothers and sisters that as warm as her father was, he was also extremely demanding and perfectionistic. Consequently, these qualities sometimes got in the way of his relationships with his friends and business colleagues.

As this daughter has built a better picture of what her father was really like, she has gradually begun to develop her own independent ideas. She's finding that she can focus more on a productive relationship with her husband.

A man I know lived more than a thousand miles from his mother and was rarely in touch with her, but his childhood relationship with her still exercised a tremendous negative influence on his life. In earlier years, his mother had often put burdensome demands on him to do chores around the house, and his father invariably backed her up. As a result of these obligations, the son felt that he had too little time to himself. He believed that his extracurricular life and even his studies suffered, and he came to harbor tremendous resentment.

When he married, this son resisted doing anything at all around the house. In fact, when his wife asked him to do even a little chore, such as take out the garbage or drive their son a short distance for a Saturday morning haircut, he would typically refuse. Sometimes, he would even respond with abusive or disrespectful language.

As we discussed this problem and some of the others

that were confronting this couple, it became evident that the husband was not reacting to his wife. He was, in fact, responding to his mother's voice, which he somehow heard being communicated through his wife. Even though he had had little or no contact with his parents as an adult, they still had a tremendous influence on him.

Once this man recognized what was happening, he was in a position to deal more constructively with the problem. First, he and his wife began to analyze their negative interactions more, especially when he could identify "Mom's voice" in what his wife said. Then, he could respond more to his wife on her own terms.

He also made a point of reestablishing contact with his mother and father through a number of phone calls and visits. In this way, he discovered that they really weren't the demanding, unreasonable martinets that he had remembered. Perhaps they were more inclined to be reasonable with him now that he was a more forceful, articulate adult. In any case, he developed a more mature, sensitive understanding of Mom and Dad—and he found he heard less and less the echoes of the "old Mom's" voice in his wife.

In this situation, as in many others like it, it was necessary for the husband first to recognize the family patterns that were being played out. Then, he could begin to move beyond the dependent love–hate emotional attachment that he had to his parents. He became freer to establish a new relationship with them and also to begin to deal with his wife as a wife, not as a substitute mother.

*Beware of cutting off your parents completely.* Somewhat paradoxically, I've discovered in my counseling that those who completely cut off their parents may find that they actually come under the influence of Mom and Dad more than ever.

One man, Bob, told me, "I've left my parents completely! I haven't seen them in years, thank heavens! They're no longer a part of my life."

But in fact, they *were* still a part of his life. As it happened, he was reproducing family patterns by reacting against what he perceived as the neglect of his mother and father. His family background reflected a classic "pendulum-swing" operation of the Dependent Love Pattern.

Specifically, Bob's grandparents, and especially his grandmother, had been overinvolved in his mother's life. As a result, Bob's mom had developed an excessive dependency on her parents. In the process, she had failed to acquire the coping skills and self-confidence that she needed to become a more competent adult.

Then the pendulum swung in the opposite direction. Bob's mom had done a 180-degree turn with her own children, including Bob. She had moved toward a hands-off approach, to the point that she gave Bob and his brothers and sisters too little direction. Bob's father had also been emotionally distant. Consequently, Bob had grown up feeling that his parents really weren't that concerned about him.

Those feelings of neglect made Bob hostile toward his parents, so much so that he decided he really didn't want to have anything more to do with them. He greatly resented the fact that, as he put it, "they did practically nothing to provide me with any significant advantages or skills as a child."

Consequently, as a father, Bob was swinging back too far in the other direction. He had become a kind of "smothering father," monitoring his children's every move. Along with his wife, he made them feel completely loved, but he didn't help them develop the sense of confidence and independence that would make them competent adults.

As a result of our discussions, Bob realized that cutting off his relationship with his parents hadn't eliminated the strong influence of his own family patterns. In fact, he had "cemented" them even more firmly into his life. It became important for him to reestablish contact with his mother and father in order to change the patterns that had become hardened into unhealthy extremes. In a series of conversations with his parents, he began to work through those relationships. At the same time, he and his wife adjusted their relationships with their children, so that his own family wouldn't be smothered with overinvolvement.

In short, "leaving" your parents doesn't mean eliminating contact with them. "Leaving," in a balanced, healthy sense, means being able to make decisions independently of them. It means being able to become an adult in your relationship with your parents, a position that involves neither doing everything they say nor reacting against everything they say.

If you find yourself approaching your mother or father as a preschooler or teenager, your challenge is not to find ways to shut off relations with them but to move into a grown-up relationship. If you can become a real adult with your parents, you'll find that you're finally free to understand them and build your own marriage and family life on firmer ground.

## The Leaving-and-Cleaving Quiz

Even if you understand the principles and examples I've provided for "leaving" your parents, you may still be wondering, "Have I really completely 'left' my parents? Are there still steps I should take, or loose ends I can tie up, to complete the process of leaving, which is so necessary for intimate cleaving?"

To test where you stand in this process of "leaving-and-cleaving," read over the following quiz. There are eight situations, each of which you should think about for a few moments to see if you can identify in them any attitude or behavior that resembles your own. Some of these illustrations are similar to cases described elsewhere in the book, and others are completely new.

*Situation #1:* When Mary gets mad at her husband, she usually calls her mother to discuss her frustrations.

*Situation #2:* Jill feels her husband John talks too harshly when they have an argument, so she will often escape even talking by going to visit her parents, who try to keep peace at all costs.

*Situation #3:* Because they wanted to save money for a house, Jane and Frank moved in with Frank's parents when they were first married. Both couples eat together every night, and Jane feels funny about trying to arrange an occasion where she can just cook dinner for just Frank. She's also uncomfortable with the idea of going down into the basement to watch television rather than watching on the set upstairs with the entire family.

*Situation #4:* Sam's parents have gone out of their way to help him and his wife get off the ground in their marriage and their careers. The parents have helped them out with their food costs and allowed them to stay at a very low rent in an apartment owned by the parents. In general, the parents have helped "the kids" out whenever they have an extra need. In fact, Mom and Dad have been so nice that Sam and his wife feel they're not in a position to object when the parents drop in unexpectedly on them—as they often do.

*Situation #5:* When George's mother comes to visit, she often rearranges certain things in the house because, as she says, "They just look better that way." George's wife resents this involvement in the physical set-up of her home, and she's asked George to take the initiative in doing something about it. But George is not about to say anything to his mom or get involved in any other way.

*Situation #6:* Liz's parents don't think that her husband, Earl, gives her enough money for clothes. So they periodically slip her a little extra cash on the side, though no one tells Earl about these transactions.

*Situation #7:* Sarah felt that she had worked out her marriage and mothering responsibilities rather well, especially since her mother was available to keep the children whenever Sarah requested her help. But now, her mother is in the hospital and Sarah is in a bind. She finds she doesn't have anyone else whom she really trusts to take care of the kids. As a result, she's feeling very cooped up and pressed in her homemaking duties.

*Situation #8:* When something goes wrong in Eliza's life, or when she feels particularly depressed or anxious about something, she gets a great sense of relief from calling her mother. Although she's been married to Todd for several years, she feels that neither he nor anyone else can really measure up to Mom in the ability to listen to her and support her sensitively.

## WHAT DOES THIS QUIZ MEAN?

All of the examples illustrate difficulties that adult children may have in leaving their parents and cleaving to their spouse. Here, in a little more detail, are some explanations.

*Don't run home to mom.* The first two examples illustrate the temptation you may feel to go to your parents for sympathy when your spouse frustrates you. Of course, every married couple has arguments. But when you do have an argument, the conflict should be worked out with your spouse directly. If you need support, get it from friends, *not* your parents.

Telling your parents and other family members too much about your marital difficulties may draw them too much into your affairs. Such parental involvement can make it hard, if not impossible, for you to "leave" them in the best sense of the word. If your family members tend to take your side rather than your spouse's, you may perpetuate a tendency for them to see you as the "good one" and your mate as the "bad one." Such an attitude will prevent your family from treating your spouse as a part of their extended relationships. Instead, they may come to look upon your mate as a kind of "outlaw."

*Establish clear boundaries.* Situations 3 and 4 illustrate the need to establish boundaries in your relationships with your parents and in-laws. In fact, you can live in the same house with your parents and still maintain your own identity as a separate couple. But boundaries are an especially important part of upholding this sense of identity.

For example, there's definitely a need for boundaries—or rules of conduct—if parents feel that they can come or go into the children's living areas without calling, knocking, or checking to see if they're welcome. Somehow, parents must understand that they have to be invited before they can enter the space of a child or child-in-law.

As an adult child, you must have your own home, apartment, separate room and keys, just as younger children should have doors on their rooms that they can close for privacy. Remember: In enmeshed, overinvolved devoted families, there sometimes tends to be a blurring of personal roles and a lack of respect for the individual needs and privacy of family members. Clear-cut, explicit boundaries about privacy and the acceptable places and means of personal interaction are essential to give married adult children the individual identity they need.

*Address attacks on your marriage or spouse directly.* The two families in situations 5 and 6 illustrate the need for an adult child to deal directly with his own parents when, in subtle and blatant ways, they attack his spouse. If you do not object when your parents criticize your spouse, you may be giving your parents priority over your mate. That's a sure indication that you've not fully "left" your parents and "cleaved" to your husband or wife.

Rather than ignoring your parents' challenges, use these as an opportunity to respond directly as an adult to your parents. If their attack is a criticism of you or your marriage, then speak up for yourself or your choices as a couple clearly. If the attack is directly on your mate, ask your parents to talk with your mate directly, *not* through you, about their concerns.

Of course, if you support your spouse, that doesn't mean you're ignoring his or her faults or playing dumb to real problems in your relationship. It simply means you are upholding your commitment to your marriage partner. Then, you and your mate can feel free and secure to go off by yourselves and work out your problems openly and directly with one another in private.

On the other hand, if you let your family criticize your spouse without addressing the criticism directly, that attitude suggests a couple of serious things about your marriage relationship. First of all, you'll be bowing to your parents' authority and relating to them as a child rather than an adult. Second, you'll in effect be saying, "I can't deal with my own spouse effectively myself, so I need somebody on my side to help me out."

*Develop peer support.* The last two examples illustrate situations in which a married child has not developed sufficient peer relationships. Instead, he or she depends primarily on Mom for support.

In the babysitting example, the daughter had not cultivated friends or child-care help that would have enabled her to live more independently. Her problem remained submerged until her mother was physically no longer available to help her.

Don't misunderstand my point here: It's wonderful that many mothers do have help from their parents in their child rearing, and the bonds between grandchildren and grandparents can be quite special. However, an adult child shouldn't rely on parents to provide the only support relationship for child rearing, and the parental relationship should not replace close peer relationships.

Once you have dealt with "leaving," you will be freer to devote your energies to "cleaving." Because you are from a strong, caring family, you probably have learned many of the skills needed for building closeness. You just may not have applied them fully to your spouse! Or perhaps you've given up too easily when you find your spouse has different ideas of how to be intimate.

Because your mate comes from a different family and is a distinct individual, cleaving will take plenty of patient communication and problem solving. You will need commitment, free of family meddling. You'll also need creativity to find ways to blend your two styles of relating into a marriage relationship that is complementary, rather than conflictual.

The goal is not to cut off your parents and other family members or develop your own isolated and independent relationship, but to give up being a dependent child with your parents and focus on your marriage as first priority. Only then can you build healthy, extended family relationships as a married adult. As you begin taking on the attitude and responsibilities of a grown adult, you can eliminate destructive dependency while enjoying the strengths of genuine caring family relationships.

# Chapter 10

# THE PERPETUAL CHILD

Most parents are a bit saddened as they see their sons and daughters growing physically bigger, becoming emotionally more mature, and beginning to exercise their own independent judgment. How often I've heard parents of growing children say: "It won't be long now—just a few more years and he'll be off on his own." Or, "I don't know what I'll do when I lose my baby!"

Yet growth, development, and independence—when the child begins a life of his own—are what the human experience is all about. On one level, parents may wish that they could have their babies forever. But when babies grow up, parents quickly begin to realize that they *don't* want them around the house on the same terms as infants and toddlers. At some point, they realize that they won't be around forever to care for their children. Their children will need to be equipped to live productively even after their parents are no longer there.

Unfortunately, however, the children in some families never grow sufficiently to strike off on their own and separate themselves successfully from Mom and Dad. They grow up physically, but they don't grow up emotionally. These adult-children remain dependent and irresponsible. They look like grown-ups, but they still act like children. In short, the son or daughter who becomes seriously emotionally debilitated as a result of the Dependent Love Pattern in an overcaring family may turn into what I call a "perpetual child."

What are some of the characteristics of this perpetual child? He or she is easily recognizable as an adult child who is still primarily dependent on his or her parents or on other parent substitutes in some major way. The dependency may involve help with housing, jobs, money, or emotional support.

Of course, many children who have been subject to the pattern display characteristics of ongoing childishness in their behavior and relationships. But when the pattern has been deeply ingrained in a family, many adult children may have become so dependent that they simply can't function without their parents or parent substitutes.

In most cases, adult children in such a situation find they're unable to achieve significant success in their jobs or to carry on meaningful adult relationships. They're always looking over their shoulders toward their parents for imagined or actual direction, support, and approval.

For example, the child may be unemployed or constantly quit or change jobs. Or if she has a job, she may not pay her own way—that is, to cover her rent, food, or transportation—because the job is inadequate or she spends money irresponsibly. The parent, or sometimes another convenient adult, will become a source of some financial support.

When the perpetual child visits home, he may expect his mother to do his laundry, cook all his meals, clean up after him, and mend his clothes. In general, he wants her to take care of him just as she did when he was a young child.

Even if a child of this type is living outside his parents' home and trying to maintain a separate marriage and family life, he and his family may still often come under the control or influence of his parents. For example, he may have to call Mom or Dad daily or at least several times a week to seek advice on even minor daily decisions. Or he may spend every spare hour and holiday in his parents' presence.

Adult children who have not "cut the apron strings" may live in an apartment or home owned by Mom or Dad, where they pay a rent far below the going rates. Or Mom or Dad may go frequently to the perpetual child's home or apartment, bringing food and doing housework or fix-it chores.

Often, perpetual children continue to live at home. In that environment, they maintain many of the same physical arrangements as well as attitudes and relationships that existed when they were much younger.

These characteristics provide us with a general idea of what's involved with an adult who is entrapped in a state of ongoing childhood. To understand better what perpetual childhood is like, it's necessary to take a closer look at some real people who have become enmeshed in this destructive state of dependent love.

To show you what I'm thinking about, let me introduce you to three people who turned into perpetual children. The first is an older teenager, the second is a twenty-five-year-old man, and the third is a forty-three-year-old woman.

*Susan, the teenage toddler.* Up until adolescence, nineteen-year-old Susan seemed in many ways to be the model child. The eldest of three children, she had good grades, did what she was told by her parents and teachers, and on the surface at least, seemed on the fast track to success.

But when Susan and her mother, Rhoda, came in to see me I could tell that something was seriously wrong beneath the surface. First of all, Susan had encountered a host of problems when she became a teenager: she had completely lost interest in her education during junior high school. Before long, she started cutting classes, taking drugs, and getting involved in sex with a variety of her male classmates.

For a while, Susan had been able to hide these activities from her parents. By the time she moved on to high school, they knew they had a problem. For one thing, her grades dropped precipitously. Finally, she failed her junior year, and when she came in to see me, she still hadn't earned enough credits to graduate.

Susan's mother and father, deeply distressed and frustrated by her behavior, told her, "Susan, if you're not going to go to school, then you *have* to get a job! We're just not going to put up with your irresponsible attitude and the lazy way you're acting!"

So Susan got a job. In fact, she got four or five jobs, one right after the other, and she lost each within a few weeks or months after she had started them. To top it all off, Susan, who lived at home, continued to hang around with a fast, sexually promiscuous, drug-oriented crowd. More than once, her parents discovered various drugs in her possession.

What was the source of Susan's problem?

As we discussed the background of this family, it became apparent that her mother, Rhoda, had given Susan very little responsibility or freedom as she was growing up. Rhoda tended to be a nagger. This characteristic came out even as the two of them were sitting in my office. Rhoda would say, "Susan, the least you can do is sit up straight while we're in this meeting!"

Throughout her life, Susan had been the object of constant nagging, pleading, and unsolicited advice. Rhoda had gotten into the habit of doing everything imaginable for Susan and her other two children: She cooked all the meals and cleaned the entire house, including the children's rooms. Even though she constantly complained, she always did the job.

Rhoda had often done part or all of her youngsters'

homework. When Susan had gone out job hunting, Rhoda had combed the want ads and mapped out a precise strategy about how prospective employers should be contacted.

Rhoda's husband, Bill, was as underinvolved as Rhoda was overinvolved. Certainly, he made a good living and paid all the bills. But Bill preferred to pursue outside interests, such as volunteering at the local political club or going out with the guys, rather than spend time with his family. As time went on, the situation worsened. When Susan got into more difficulty with her schoolwork and social life, Bill tended to play down the problem by saying, "All teenagers get into trouble!" Or, "Her teachers are terrible—what do you expect!" Then he withdrew further into his own interests. In fact, Bill was so distant that he resisted for several weeks even coming in to meet me and discuss his family's problems.

Clearly, this was a classic case of the Dependent Love Pattern, with an overinvolved mother, an underinvolved father, and overly dependent children. In fact, there were signs that Susan's brother might soon join her in perpetual childhood. As the middle child who was just reaching his teenage years, this boy was also starting to show signs of underachievement at school and rebellion at home. As for the youngest child, a nine-year-old daughter, she seemed to be doing rather well in school and in her home life. But at that age, so had Susan! Obviously, given the family history, there could be no guarantees about how any of these kids would turn out.

To get the full picture, I explored the types of families that Rhoda and Bill had come from. Sure enough, their answers provided the remaining pieces of the emotional jigsaw puzzle. Rhoda had been the eldest child whose mother had treated her in much the same way as she was treating Susan. In fact Rhoda usually called her mother once a day for advice and guidance about her own child rearing.

Bill had also grown up in a family where his mother

had exercised an unusually dominant role and his father was mostly a background figure. Obviously, both Bill and Rhoda had responded to their parent's examples and were now replaying a similar family "tape" in their own home.

In effect, then, the Dependent Love Pattern in this family had turned Susan into a perpetual child at the age of nineteen. Furthermore, it was clear that if we didn't take steps immediately to try to adjust the situation, she might be locked into this pattern for many years—perhaps even the rest of her life. But what could be done?

We all agreed that Rhoda's nagging, excessive control and overconcern toward her children didn't work. Moreover, doing her children's homework and trying to manage Susan's job-hunting strategy had backfired: The children's grades had plummeted, and Susan couldn't hold a job even when she found one.

Our approach zeroed in on the difficulties in the family relationships. The first step was to get both parents involved to even the balance in their child rearing and start them talking and working together. I asked them to work out a few basic rules and to establish consequences for the kids who failed to observe the rules. This project alone took a great deal of work because the couple had started out so far apart, with such different approaches to their family responsibilities.

I also encouraged Rhoda to take a break from her onerous duties by no longer doing things for the grown children. Instead, I urged her to develop her own friends and activities away from her home and away from her parents. We began by spending about a half hour brainstorming and discussing activities and friends that she could work at cultivating.

Along with this, I asked Bill to play the heavy hand in enforcing the new family rules that he and Rhoda had agreed upon. Because he had been in the background so long, we had to discuss carefully just what might keep him from this task and how to overcome the old patterns.

Of course, none of this was easy, especially for Rhoda. When a smothering mother loses her job, in the sense of not having as much to do for her children, a great vacuum may appear in her life. She found it difficult to keep her resolution to play a smaller part in the lives of her children. Furthermore, it wasn't easy for her to embark on new outside projects and relationships. Rhoda realized, though, the importance of helping Susan to become more independent. She did her best to keep out of Susan's affairs, to move on with her own life, and to abide by the guidelines we had established.

As for Bill, my asking him to take an active role at home was like asking him to learn a new sport. He didn't really know how to begin, and his moves felt very awkward at first. But with coaching, he became quite adept and even learned to enjoy family life.

As Rhoda and Bill joined together as parents, the children weren't able to play the two of them off against one another anymore. Consequently, Susan actually began to ''grow up,'' in the sense that she developed more independence and more of a sense of her own identity. The changes in this family are still very much in process. Susan is doing much better, her younger brother has overcome some of his problems at school and at home, and the outlook is bright for the younger daughter.

In any event, Susan and perhaps her siblings have avoided the more deeply ingrained dependency situation of an older young man named Tom.

*Tom, the overgrown mama's boy.* Tom, twenty-five-years old, was the youngest of four children. He had been asthmatic as a child, and that, coupled with being the family's only son, had caused his mother, Louise, to give him special, overattentive care. His three older sisters, despite the squabbling they engaged in among themselves, saw Tom as their own ''doll-baby'' brother. In effect, this family situation gave him the advantage—or disadvantage, as it turned out—of having three extra "mothers" to smother him.

This intense interest in Tom was not shared by his father. Dad had been looking for a strapping, athletic son, and Tom didn't seem to have many inclinations in this direction. As a result, the father more or less ignored the son and left him to the tender mercies of the females in the family. Dad was most at home either fighting with Louise or taking a drink and retiring to the TV room.

Almost inevitably, Tom developed a dependency on his mother and sisters to make decisions and get things done for him. Interestingly enough, his sisters were much more independent, perhaps because there were too many of them for Louise to focus her attention on only one. Consequently, the girls developed into rather strong-willed young women, and they went on to do well in their school work, to launch successful careers, and to become involved in normal marriages.

Tom wasn't so lucky. His major problems came to the fore when he was only about twelve years old because it was at that time that his father left home and asked Louise for a divorce. Louise, who had been a devoted wife as well as an extremely attentive mother, was shocked and devastated by this turn of events.

At first, she sank into a deep depression, completely immobilized by the loss of her husband and the apparent end of her dreams of creating an ideal family environment. Then, realizing she had to get on with her life and take care of her son, who was the only child still living full-time at home, she focused all her attention on Tom.

Tom became, in a sense, a substitute husband for Louise, as she confided in him all her frustrations, doubts, and dreams. Because he had been conditioned to depend on her or his sisters for so much, Tom slipped naturally into this dual role as son and surrogate husband for his mother.

Perhaps to demonstrate his important position in her life, Louise wouldn't allow him to lift a finger around the house. "Oh, you let me do that, Tom!" she would say. "You have better things to do than women's work!"

When the normal time arrived to leave for college as his sisters had, Tom chose instead to go to a small junior college in his home town, mainly because he didn't want to go away from home and leave his mother alone. Predictably, she encouraged him to stay because the relationship had grown so close. As for Tom, he was afraid that she wouldn't be able to function without him. He was also afraid that he wouldn't be able to function without her, after all the catering and pampering he had received.

Tom was quite friendly and appeared to have many friends, but in fact, he felt more comfortable with his mother than with his peers. Never having identified with his father, he experienced some sexual confusion. Consequently, he tried to avoid intimate relationships while still maintaining an external cordiality with others.

Tom lived at home during his entire college experience. Then, when he was finally ready to get a job, he told his mother, "You know, I think I'd like to start my own business and maybe run it out of the home here. I don't think I'm really suited to work for somebody else."

Louise readily agreed and even volunteered to put up some of her savings to help him get started. Tom proceeded to rely on his mother at every step as he set the business up and made crucial marketing decisions. Between the two of them, with their lack of experience, the operation soon failed.

Even after the collapse of their venture, the two continued their inseparable ways, apparently with no hard feelings or recriminations. Still living with his mother, Tom got a part-time job in town, which he held for a few months and then finally quit after his mother suggested that it wasn't up to his standards. Of course, Tom felt no financial pressure from being out of work because his mother always provided him with a place to stay and covered his expenses.

Eventually things began to go wrong in their living arrangement. All was not completely rosy in the little nest that Louise and Tom had created for themselves— for several reasons. Quite naturally, Tom sensed that something was wrong with his life. He had no career, no friends, no source of real fulfillment. Because there was no one else around to blame, he started taking his frustrations out on his mother. They got into increasingly intense arguments, apparently over nothing—to the point, at times, of violence.

Louise, quite rightly, also perceived that something was seriously wrong with their relationship. She knew that she loved her son deeply, and she was equally certain that he loved her. So why was he lashing out at her in these angry bursts of hostility?

Louise finally came to me for help when she realized that Tom's life seemed to be going nowhere, and that neither of them could figure out what was wrong. As we talked, Louise began to see some of the difficulties produced by Tom's smothered family experience, and she began to see some painful steps that she would have to take.

First of all, I encouraged Louise to confront the fact that she had never really resolved her broken marriage. "You need to recognize that relationship is over and then go through a grieving process, much as you grieve over the death of a loved one," I told her.

To be sure, she needed companionship and support, but getting it primarily from her son was exacting a high emotional price from both of them. It was important for her to stop focusing so much on caring for her grown son—who had turned into a perpetual child—and to develop other relationships and interests.

Finally, I recommended that Louise allow Tom to stand on his own two feet in any future business ventures or job efforts. If he failed, then he should fail on his own terms. She shouldn't be there to bail him out or provide a safety net. The only way he was going to learn to be independent was to take a few hard knocks and learn some of the tough facts of life by trial and error.

Tom came in for many of our sessions, and together, the three of us worked out a strategy. For one thing, Tom began to separate himself in healthy ways from his mother and finally even moved out of her home and got his own apartment. Interestingly enough, as he and his mother separated, they actually had a better relationship than when they had lived together, with their arguments and occasional violent outbursts.

In addition, as part of the healing process, I encouraged Tom to seek out his father, who had remarried and was living a few hours' drive away. As it happened, his father had given up trying to establish a relationship with Tom because of the close attachment the boy had to his mother. But when Dad learned that his son was interested in repairing their relationship, he was eager to respond as best he could, given the responsibilities he had with his new family.

Tom was a few years older than the teenager, Susan, whom we considered previously, but both were relatively young when I met them and were at the beginning of a perpetual child problem. At the far end of the spectrum, a person may remain a perpetual child well into middle age and even older—unless steps are taken earlier to correct the problem and encourage greater independence. Even at a later stage, though, beneficial change is possible.

*Pam, the middle-aged perpetual child.* Pam originally came to me because she had been suffering from serious ongoing bouts with depression. Forty-three years of age, she had been living with her mother, Marsha, all her life. This arrangement had been triggered by her mother's divorce from her father when Pam was eighteen.

At the time of the divorce, Pam had been enrolled in a secretarial school, and she had been in the process of looking for an apartment with a couple of her classmates.

The idea was that when they all graduated, they would get good jobs, pool their salaries, and rent a plush apartment in a high-rise building in the downtown area of a nearby city. After that, they expected that their social life would bloom in the city's singles community.

Even as she was making these plans, Pam had reservations. She had always been extremely close to her mother and had depended on her for emotional as well as financial support as she was growing up. How could she continue that relationship if she moved in with two other young women? When her father left her mother, Pam immediately decided that her first responsibility was to Mom. Without thinking twice, she gave up her plans with her friends and instead planned her future around Marsha.

Although Pam was quite attractive, she rarely accepted invitations for dates after moving in with Mom. She rationalized by telling herself that her mother needed her more than some young man who might express a passing sexual interest. In fact, Pam craved the nurturing and support that she had come to expect from her mother—a craving that she found no man could ever really satisfy.

Eventually, the offers for dates ceased, partly because Pam turned down so many of them and partly because she gained a lot of weight. As a result, she settled down into a stable and rather sedate relationship with her mother in which she acted as a sounding board for Marsha's various concerns. At the same time, Pam related to her mother much as she had when she was a preadolescent. Mom often helped her pick her clothes, did most of the washing and cooking, and in general acted as she had done when Pam was just a child.

Gradually, Pam's emotional state deteriorated. She found that she became tired a great deal more often than she had in the past, and she cried uncontrollably at times. She was unable to follow through on projects at work or in their church community, where both she and her mother were very active. On top of all this, she and her

mother seemed to bicker constantly, even over minor issues. In a way, their arguing was their only means of
establishing their individual identities.

As we talked, it became evident that Pam and her
mother had become far too ingrown in their relationship.
Indeed, they both needed more ''space,'' or independence and separation from each other, if they hoped to
make their relationship work. In fact, as I learned in later
sessions with Marsha present, both the mother and
daughter experienced periodic depression and near-
paralysis in their activities and relationships. They had
simply become too dependent on one another.

What was the solution to their family problems? In this
case, radical psychological or social surgery didn't seem
in order. For one thing, Pam was now middle-aged and
had no apparent prospects of or interest in marriage. In
addition, both were deeply afraid of loneliness and both
felt a need for the kind of companionship that they had
experienced all their lives. So I didn't recommend that
the mother and daughter split up and live in separate
homes or apartments.

At the same time, it was evident that they had to do
something to make their relationship healthier and more
workable. The strategy that we eventually settled on was
to set aside some time so that each could be alone or
pursue independent interests. In this way, they could each
get some of the ''space'' that they needed. At the same
time, they could maintain the best part of the mother–
daughter relationship that they had developed over decades.

Fortunately, both mother and daughter were deeply
involved in their church community. They found that they
were able to cultivate long-standing relationships with
others. Although it took some effort to get out more often
and open up to others, they were able to develop outside
relationships within the supportive family environment
of their church.

Marsha also learned to bite her tongue and let Pam go

off and shop by herself at times. And Pam learned to let her mother work on several service projects without nagging her about being out too much.

The love–hate dynamic in this mother–daughter situation was subtle, and for years the tension had remained beneath the surface. Finally, the frustration had broken through, and something had to be done about it. Otherwise, anger and bad feelings might have overwhelmed both mother and daughter. In that event, the very dependency that had joined them together might have produced a violent situation and caused deep emotional scars.

*Herb, a disabled thirty-eight-year-old.* The Dependent Love Pattern for another middle-aged child began under somewhat different circumstances. Herb was in a car accident when he was only three years old; as a result, he had lost his right arm above the elbow. Because he was the younger of two brothers, he had always been regarded as the "baby" in the family by his mother, Eleanor. His disability caused her to give him even more care and attention, in part because she felt sorry for him and in part because she felt guilty for not having somehow protected him during the car accident. So Eleanor consistently went overboard in doing things for Herb, even though he could have done many of them himself.

Of course, Herb did face challenges ordinary kids don't encounter. For example, he had extra trouble learning to dress himself because of his missing arm. It took him a little longer than other boys to pick up things in his room and do other personal tasks. Eleanor, beset by sympathy and remorse, tried to make it up to Herb by doing everything for him. As a result, the boy failed to develop many of the basic skills of daily life. Soon, he came to expect that others would care for him and look after him, down to the most minute details of his existence.

Unfortunately, Herb's father never stepped in to break up the emerging Dependent Love Pattern. For one thing, he had developed a partiality toward his older son, Ben, who, like the father, was more athletically inclined. The father found it difficult to relate to Herb because few of the boy's interests seemed to coincide with his. As Eleanor poured more and more of herself into Herb and less into her husband except through criticism, the father became more and more detached from his younger son, both emotionally and physically. Consequently, Herb gravitated more and more into the orbit of his mother's smothering love.

This pattern, which had begun early in Herb's life, deepened progressively as he grew older. By the time he was a teenager, he was involved in problems with heavy drinking and serious misbehavior at school and in the community. In fact, Herb was arrested on two occasions, once for drunken driving and once for vandalizing a neighbor's home. In both instances, his mother helped to bail him out by hiring an expensive lawyer.

As Herb emerged from his teenager years, his dependence on his mother increased. He attended a local college for a year or so, but then quit to get a job. He couldn't hold the job, and after a series of failures he concluded that "nobody wants to hire a cripple." He began to spend most of his time around home—when he wasn't out drinking and carousing with his friends.

During this time, the parent's marriage relationship deteriorated to the point that Herb's father finally left home. There had never been good communication between the parents. In the father's view, another major source of contention between them had been the mother's smothering relationship with the younger son.

"You treat that boy like a baby!" Mom quoted Dad as saying. "You won't let him grow up!"

In subsequent years, Herb did leave home, sometimes for months at a time, with the announced intention of finding a job in another city. But he would always write to his mother for money, and he always eventually returned to her. Finally, when it looked like he had come back home to stay at the age of thirty-eight, Eleanor realized that she had a major problem on her hands—one she didn't feel able to handle by herself. So she came to me for advice.

As we talked, it became evident that Eleanor was still treating Herb like a little child. She totally accepted all his behavior, no matter how outrageous it was. He might come in roaring drunk at 3:00 A.M., but she put up with it because he was her "little boy." In fact, he really wasn't a little boy, and soon she found that his misbehavior was completely disrupting her home and personal life.

Eleanor had a small apartment and liked to invite her friends over for coffee or to watch television, but Herb, just like an unruly preschooler, somehow managed to live all over the house. His clothes, magazines, beer cans, and other paraphernalia were strewn from the kitchen, across the living room, and back to his bedroom. Sometimes he even tossed his dirty clothes into her room so that she would be sure to clean them.

What were the other son and father doing at this time? The father had remarried and had other children by his new wife. Eleanor was certain that he "couldn't care less" about what was going on with Herb and her. He never communicated with either of them and had even let Herb know he wasn't interested in establishing a relationship. On one occasion, when Herb had dropped in on him unexpectedly, Dad had been rather abrupt, cutting the visit short. While Herb was there, the father seemed to try to spend as little time as possible with him.

Herb's brother, Ben, had moved away to another state, where he was pursuing an independent life with his own family. But unlike his father, Ben had welcomed Herb into his home on a couple of occasions. "Uncle Herb" had gone over quite well in several outings with his older brother's children.

Still, Herb's main base of operations remained Eleanor's apartment. In effect, the dependent son had completely taken over the smothering mother's life—all because a Dependent Love Pattern, involving all the family members over a period of several decades, had become a dominant force in this family.

It was obvious that Eleanor would never be able to throw Herb abruptly out of the house or to take any other really tough stands with him. Their dependent relationship had gone on for too long to make such a quick and total separation possible. On the other hand, it was also obvious that the current situation couldn't continue because Eleanor had already been practically pushed out of her own home.

We began to build a new family strategy on a middle ground. The objective was to allow Eleanor to maintain her relationship with Herb and yet help him to go through a growing-up process that he had missed earlier in life. First of all, Eleanor had to realize that the excessive attention she had given Herb—attention arising from her concern about his disability—had in fact given him additional handicaps. He had become emotionally as well as physically incapacitated because of the Dependent Love Pattern that prevailed in his family.

When Eleanor came to see me, she was already feeling intense frustration and a considerable amount of hostility toward her son. These emotions made her feel even guiltier than she had before. "I know I shouldn't feel this way, but I just can't help myself!" she told me.

I assured her that, given the way the relationships in her family had developed, there was every reason for her to feel as she did. The challenge now was to change the patterns of action that had produced those feelings. She and other family members had to take steps to readjust the family relationships so that Herb could develop into a more independent adult.

Specifically, we mapped out a set of family rules that stated clearly what Herb and Eleanor could expect of one another. During later sessions when Herb began to participate in the counseling, the two of them agreed that he would clean up his things around the house, he would not drink at all in the house, and he would always get home by a certain hour.

If Herb failed to live up to these responsibilities, Eleanor would automatically take certain countermeasures. For example, if Herb wasn't home by a certain hour, she would lock the door and he would have to sleep elsewhere. If he failed to pick up his things from around the house, she would be justified in gathering them up into a pile and throwing them in the middle of the floor in his room.

As you might expect, given the long-term nature of the dependent relationship between Eleanor and Herb, these changes didn't go completely smoothly. The first few times that Herb got home late, Eleanor couldn't bring herself to lock him out. When she tried to reprimand him, he became abusive and started screaming at the top of his lungs. Eventually, she resolved to stick by the rules we had agreed to. As painful as it was for her, she did keep the door locked the next time Herb came home after hours, despite the fact that he banged on it for five or ten minutes.

As she worked on these changes, Eleanor found that she needed outside support and help. She learned to open up to some friends in a prayer group she attended at church. During their conversations, she asked these women to help her stand firm in her new approach.

The older son, Ben, turned out to be an encouragement to Herb as he saw Herb trying to make real changes. They began actually to relate and help each other as brothers rather than as competing companions for their mother.

Eleanor and her family are still trying to break completely free of the Dependent Love Pattern, but they're making good progress. By setting and expecting realistic limits and responsibilities for the dependent child, they are all working toward a more equal set of relationships that will be satisfying to everyone concerned.

In short, people who are physically or emotionally

handicapped like Herb don't have to be relegated to the role of the perpetual child. To be sure, the presence of a handicap can make it more likely that a family, even an otherwise balanced one, will develop a Dependent Love Pattern. But with extra encouragement and a step-by-step teaching of necessary skills, there's no reason why the disabled child shouldn't grow up. He can become just as competent and self-confident as those without special problems.

Obviously, these are some difficult and extreme situations that involve perpetual children. To whatever extent this condition exists, it's important for family members to begin to tackle it now, before it gets any worse. We've already seen the ways that some parents and children have started moving toward a more balanced and independent relationship with one another. Now, let me describe in a little more detail what roles parents can play in helping the perpetual child escape the dilemma.

## What Can Mom and Dad Do?

The first indication that there's something wrong in a family—that a perpetual child has emerged full-blown from a deeply ingrained dependency pattern—often comes from the parents.

To be sure, parents often get a great deal of pleasure out of coddling and cuddling and smothering and snuggling their special son or daughter. But as Junior grows older, the smothering becomes a lot less fun. In fact, a son's or daughter's excessive dependence on the mother, in particular, can become downright burdensome, especially when the child moves into adolescence and finally into adulthood. In more extreme situations, it's usually the parent who comes to the counselor complaining about the oppressive family situation.

The solution is not simply a matter of having Mom back off and demand that the children take on more responsibility, although that may be a piece of the solution.

Step one is for the parents to address their differences with each other, rather than communicating through the children. When the conflicts are as severe as those in most families with perpetual children, this step is usually best taken with the help of a professional family therapist.

Step two is for Dad to enter into the parenting and take more responsibility for the child's well-being. He must advise and guide the perpetual child out of his dilemma and support Mom as she tries to extricate herself from the smothering behavior she may have been displaying. In short, Dad must become a less distant figure and must become a very real, active player in the family scene.

## What Mom Can Do by Herself

If both parents are willing to make an effort to change the situation, the prospects for the child will be much brighter, no matter what his age. But too often, only one parent is willing to make the effort—and it's usually the mother.

On too many occasions, Dad is quite happy to have Mom continue to be overburdened with the child's problems, because he has ''other fish to fry,'' other interests and responsibilities that seem more important than parenting. Or his own problems—for example, drinking or abusive anger—may be serious ones that he isn't aware of or isn't willing to address.

If Dad refuses to play an active role or if he seems unable to participate to the extent necessary, Mom will have to look to outside sources for help. In a divorce situation, or even a marriage that seems destined to be forever unfulfilling, a wife will need to work to resolve her own anger, as well as find appropriate sources of critically needed support and companionship. Let me emphasize that the mother *must* get some sort of support system to reinforce her efforts. If she tries to act completely on her own, the chances are she'll fail and the

Dependent Love Pattern will prevail indefinitely in the family.

Fortunately, there are a number of alternatives that can provide Mom with some help as she tries to operate without her husband's support. For example, many churches, clubs, and businesses have informal prayer-and-share groups. In these gatherings, those from common religious backgrounds get together, discuss their problems—including family difficulties—and receive advice and support from like-minded believers. Particularly helpful are self-help groups that focus specifically on helping families in handling children's difficulties, like Families Anonymous. Finally, professional family therapists are available for help with just these sorts of problems. Only with such support can Mom take the difficult steps of actually stopping the doing-for, the bailing-out, and other types of behavior that support an adult child's irresponsibility.

Whether Mom is working with Dad or with others, the process of parental withdrawal from overinvolvement is best carried out in small, preannounced steps, which you know you can accomplish. For example, you may announce and then follow through with no longer doing the children's laundry and cooking for the entire family only on Saturdays. Or, if your child is living at home you might begin by actually charging a full, market-level rent rather than saying you're going to kick the kids out without following through on the threat.

Remember not to try to solve these problems completely on your own. An extremely strong, motivated person can certainly make progress in dealing with a perpetual child. Chances are you'll do the best, most complete job—and see the greatest changes among your loved ones—if you establish links with other family members or outside sources of support.

# Part IV

# STRATEGIES

# Chapter 11

# BREAKING FREE FROM THE DEPENDENT LOVE PATTERN

Changing personal habits is hard. When those habits are deeply ingrained in family relationships—when the behavior of one person depends to a significant degree on the responses and attitudes of others—meaningful change can sometimes seem impossible to achieve.

Yet, the dependency of each person on the reactions of the others actually gives one person *more* leverage for positive change because the actions of only one person can make a tremendous difference, as they ripple through surrounding relationships. I'm reminded of that great Frank Capra film, *It's a Wonderful Life*, starring Jimmy Stewart, who showed through his character that one person can change not only his family's future, but also the future of the surrounding community.

In this movie, Stewart was on the verge of committing suicide because he felt his life had been a complete waste. But an angel intervened and proceeded to show him what a tremendous positive effect he had achieved in little ways as he had interacted over the years in the lives of others.

A similar experience may occur in families who are

enmeshed in a destructive Dependent Love Pattern. When Mom has smothered her youngsters for years, when Dad has grown emotionally distant, and when the children have become overly dependent, the situation may seem overwhelming. In fact, you may feel things are completely hopeless when you realize that your family behaviors are rooted in generational patterns that can be traced to grandparents and even earlier ancestors.

Of course, I often hear objections from a mother or child who can't seem to get anyone else in the family to participate. "What can I do without the cooperation of the whole family?" the frustrated individuals may ask.

It's quite true that the best solution in a family with serious dependency problems will involve everyone. All members should pitch in and work on the problems. But it's also true that one individual can often get things started—and can have a big impact. In this regard, I think of family members as pool balls, scattered here and there on a pool table. If there's no movement on the table, then the balls are going to stay just where they are. But if you roll one ball firmly against another and initiate a ricochet action, the configuration of those balls in relation to one another is going to change immediately. It only took movement by one ball to get everything started!

Similarly, you as an individual in your family can get things started if you'll just begin to take certain steps that promote helpful change and less dependency. The first step in achieving beneficial change with your loved ones is for you to find a confidant.

## Find a Confidant

A few strong people can identify a problem, become motivated, and launch and follow an action program all on their own. Most of us, though, have difficulty being objective and observing clearly when we're dealing with our own families. Often, an outsider can provide much-needed objectivity to help us see things that otherwise may escape us. We need some help and understanding to get started and follow up on a plan for change.

If you are from a devoted family, you probably function best with a companion. As you prepare to change a Dependent Love Pattern in your family, it's helpful to find a confidant who can back you up from the very beginning. Your confidant should be a person with whom you can freely share your concerns. You'll need to talk through what's bothering you and discuss the patterns you've begun to observe. Sometimes, just in the process of talking with another person, things become clearer and you can see new perspectives.

Your confidant should be a person who is able to listen as well as give objective advice and personal support. If the person is only interested in talking and interjecting his or her own family perspective and experiences into your family, you may become confused, rather than feel supported.

Perhaps the most important advantage of having a confidant is simply to have someone who knows about your plan and will help keep you on track. You need an adviser who will hold you accountable to your own goals. Periodic questions put to you by your confidant, such as, "How are you doing with your project?" can do wonders to keep you moving in the right direction. The key traits of the confidant are a simple commitment to you as a friend and a desire to see you grow as a person.

If you're married, your best confidant would usually be your spouse. Ideally, the person you are committed to "cleaving to" for the rest of your life should be your most natural supporter. By sharing openly your concerns and plans, you might very well deepen your relationship. If you have a reasonably good friendship and open lines of communication with your spouse, try him or her first as a confidant. Although your spouse won't be objective, he or she will have a valuable inside perspective. If you can begin the whole plan for family change together as a couple, you'll already be up to step two in this plan for change.

Of course, you may have great conflicts with your spouse or feel that his or her lack of involvement is your biggest problem. In that case, you may want to ask a friend to support you at first. Usually, a friend with a sensitive ear and an open heart will be more than willing to be a supporter in this venture. It's just a matter of asking clearly for help.

But you may find that you seem to have no one whom you feel comfortable asking. Or you may choose a confidant who just does not work out. Sometimes, no matter how willing your confidant, you may get to a point where you feel stuck by the particular interactions in your family. Or your family's problems may be too serious for any untrained person to handle. For example, they may involve such things as drug abuse, alcoholism, or suicidal tendencies.

In any of these cases, you may need to find a professional family therapist, at least to get you started. Such a counselor can also make the task quicker and easier if you find yourself confused about how your family works or unsure how to really take steps to change things. Remember that a family therapist's goal is not to see you forever but to be a coach for your own work in your family.

## Identify Your Specific Family Pattern

Once you've decided to work for positive change and have found a confidant to support you in the process, the next step is to try to identify your family's patterns as specifically as possible. To do this, try for a moment to be an observer, not just a participant in your family. Think about who is in your family, the overall atmosphere at home, the particular interactions among people, and what your family rules are.

Now, using the four parts of the Dependent Love Pattern, try to identify each of these in your own family:

- Who is overinvolved, and exactly with whom and how?
- Who is distant, and from whom and how?
- How is each of the children overly dependent?
- What part do grandparents play in your family? Were/are they smothering or neglectful?

The chart on page 199 will help you in writing out your observations. Be sure to think of specific examples so that you can learn to see exactly how your family patterns operate. You may want to include both things that people say and things that they do in your examples.

When you have observed all the members of your family and their roles in the Dependent Love Pattern, focus closely on what your own role is. Remember that you are the only person you can change directly. You need to be most familiar with the ways you interact with each of the other members.

## Envision and Plan Goals

Now that you have a reasonably clear picture of how you and your family interact, think about how you would like the patterns to change. Although you may want to begin by envisioning desired changes for other members of your family, you must concentrate now on changes that *you* can make.

First, write out your overall goals for change. For example, if you are a dependent adult child, you may aim to become independent of your parents financially and socially. Or if you are an overinvolved mother, you may aim to let go of your children and encourage them to move forward on their own. Stating such goals in a short, catchy phrase can be helpful. Some possibilities:

"Free to be me."

"Be my own person."

"Let go and let God."

"Retired from full-time mothering."

Next, think about your relationships with each member of your family—parents, mate, and children. For each relationship, think about what basic change you'd like, such as less dependency, more closeness, less involvement. Then, think of specific things you can say or do differently to make this change.

Now, looking at all the relationships and your desired change, pick one small action in one relationship for a first step to get the ball rolling. Don't try to move mountains or make major reforms all at once. It's better just to start with a few simple changes, which you know you can make, than to take on a monstrous task that appears to be impossible.

Write out exactly what you plan to do. Then, think of a good time to do it. When and where would it be easiest to do and most likely to work out successfully? You may find it helpful to rehearse with your confidant what you plan to say, to write it down for yourself, or to practice it in your mind a number of times.

Next, think through how the other person is likely to react. You probably can envision the worst possible outcome, so write it down and discuss with your confidant how you might respond in that situation. You may even want to try some role playing to provide some practice in how conversations might develop and how patterns of interaction might change.

Finally, follow through on your planned changes. If you find that you just can't seem to gather the courage or confidence to act with a certain individual, consider picking a first step to take with someone you find more approachable. Or consider making your first step toward change a smaller one. Don't underestimate how significant even a seemingly trivial action on your part may be! Remember: Little steps in the right direction, at a pace you're comfortable with, are what's needed. Afterward,

## Understanding the Dependent Love Pattern in your Family

| | WHO? | HOW? (GIVE EXAMPLES) |
|---|---|---|
| Overinvolved Parent | | |
| Underinvolved (or Coinvolved) Parent | | |
| Dependent Child(ren) | | |
| Grandparents: | smothering, neglectful, or harsh? | |
| Maternal | | |
| Paternal | | |

## STEPS TOWARD CHANGING MY FAMILY'S DEPENDENT LOVE PATTERN

My overall goal for change is for me to:

Specifically, my goal in my relationship with:

| | GOAL | WHAT I WILL DO DIFFERENTLY |
|---|---|---|
| Mother | | 1.<br>2.<br>3. |
| Father | | 1.<br>2.<br>3. |
| Husband/Wife | | 1.<br>2.<br>3. |
| Child(ren) | | 1.<br>2.<br>3. |
| | | 1.<br>2.<br>3. |

be sure to evaluate how your first step toward change went. It may be helpful to talk with your confidant and discuss both what went well and what needs further work.

Once you successfully take your first step, then you're ready to plan out a series of ''change steps'' to take over a period of time with each person in your family. Of course, you'll want to take one or two steps at a time, just as you did with your first attempt.

Before you work on this any further, let me share with you some of the specific steps I've found to be helpful for family members who are caught in a Dependent Love Pattern. In the next chapter, I'll give some guidance for parents who are ready to let go and let their children grow. Then, we'll discuss some ideas for children who want to end the destructive dependencies in their relationships.

PLANNING EACH STEP

Step Number _____ Planning Date _____

| | |
|---|---|
| What I will do | |
| When/Where | |
| Difficulties I may encounter | 1. 2. |
| How I will handle them | 1. 2. |
| Evaluation: What went well | |
| What needs further work | |

## Steps toward Reaching my Goal
### *(Make them small and do-able)*

Plan one step first; after doing it, plan two more; then two more; etc.

| what i will do | when (and how) |
|---|---|
| 1. | |
| 2. | |
| 3. | |
| 4. | |
| 5. | |
| 6. | |
| 7. | |

# Chapter 12

## WHAT'S A MOM OR DAD TO DO?

When a mother and father see a youngster failing to develop to full potential, the sight can be extremely painful. After all, as a devoted parent, you've put a significant part of your life into this child. Why isn't he developing into his "own person"? Why doesn't she take the lead with her peers and do what you feel she's really capable of doing?

What's a mom or dad to do?

Fortunately, there are constructive responses that you, as a parent, can make to help your child break free of the Dependent Love Pattern, grow competent, and begin to develop his or her own talents and abilities.

To be most effective, it's best for parents of dependent children to work on first things first, one step at a time. To help you in this process, I've divided the most important actions for parents into six key steps.

## Step #1:
## Resolve Your Relationship
## with Your Own Parents

In another context, we've mentioned how important it is for an adult to "leave" his parents before he can "cleave" to a spouse and create his own new, healthy family situation. If you came out of a family where one or both of your parents had a smothering attitude toward you, you should stop reading this chapter right now and skip to the next one. There, you'll see how adult children with smothering mothers, and perhaps smothering fathers, can break free of the influence of their backgrounds and grow independent. Then, when you've dealt with those issues, you'll be ready to return to this advice on parental activism.

On the other hand, if your parents were neglectful of you in some ways, you may only be able to "leave" them by resolving your feelings of anger and frustration about the way they brought you up. Then, you'll be in a position to develop a more open and productive relationship with them. Most people who have been caught up in a Dependent Love Pattern have had at least one parent whom they regarded as neglectful—usually, an emotionally distant father. Others have grown up with both parents seeming not to care that much about showing love to them or guiding or teaching them in their childhood activities.

How can you resolve any bad feelings you may have about how your parents may have neglected you, or failed to guide or teach you properly? First of all, I would suggest that you not just vent your anger toward them. Yes, you need to be aware of your own anger and its sources. But if you blow up at your parents, they may very well react in an angry or hostile way toward you—and you'll be worse off than you were before. Until you can express your hurt with some understanding, you're unlikely to see good results.

I've found the best way to begin to approach parents

who seem neglectful, uninterested, or overly permissive is first to try to gain some understanding of them. You can do this by asking some questions designed to get them to open up and talk about their own experiences and feelings. In this way, you'll promote productive communication with them. You may also learn things that will give you a better understanding of who they are and why they've acted as they have.

Some questions that will tend to open them up and also give you some very useful information are:

"What were my grandparents like?"

"How were they as parents?"

"Tell me about your mother's and your father's families."

"What was your childhood like?"

"What did you like? Dislike?"

"What problems did you face when you were growing up?"

"How did you overcome the challenges you faced in your childhood?"

"What was it like for you when you were my age?"

If you already know a lot about your parents, you may have much more specific questions in each of these areas. As you ask your mother or father these things, you should approach her or him in a curious and interested way, not blaming or being critical. Be an investigator, a historian, a detective! The more details and stories about their background you learn, the easier it will be for you to see things from their perspective and to understand how they came to be the persons and parents that they are. Don't give up if they seem reluctant to talk or if they give you one-word answers. After all, they're new at this form of communication, and you have to give them a chance to start feeling comfortable and get to know you better.

If your parents are no longer alive, you can pose these questions to aunts, uncles, or other relatives who can give you a better picture of your parents' experiences and feelings.

As you're asking these questions and beginning to understand your parents better, you may find that your own anger is decreasing. Certainly, understanding why someone hurt you or neglected you won't take away all the pain, but at least such understanding will pave the way to forgiveness in the future.

After you've done this exploratory questioning and begun to understand your parents' viewpoint, it can be helpful to write a letter that you think your mother or father might have written to you. In it, explain your parent's perspective on what happened in your family. By putting yourself in your parent's shoes, you'll find that you're able to understand your mother or father even better than simply by speaking with him or her. You'll begin to give explanations for your parent's conduct that you may never have thought about before. Also, putting a point of view on paper can encourage you to go back to that parent once again to check out your understanding and pursue your conversations in greater depth. Usually greater understanding brings reduced anger, and with less anger, you'll be free to apply your emotional energies in positive ways.

Sometimes, even with understanding, hurts remain from abuses or neglect. If so, you will need to work hard on developing new supportive healing relationships with others. You'll need to find ways to receive the nurturing you missed and to get the loving care you wish for. As an adult, you are not limited to your parents but can reach out to other resources, such as extended family members, friends, church or synagogue members, and support group participants.

With your parents you may find healing comes only after the act of forgiveness. I've encountered many adult children who tell me, "Certainly, I can *understand* where my parents are coming from. But that doesn't change what they did to me. I certainly can't forgive them!"

But think about who your anger is hurting most: It's

*you*, as you wallow in your inner turmoil and bitterness. Forgiveness enables you to become fully freed from your anger so that you can develop as good a relationship as possible with your parents. Then, you'll also be free to move forward positively in other relationships.

When I refer to forgiving, incidentally, I don't necessarily mean that you have to walk up to your own parents and say, "I forgive you." Many times, if you take such a direct approach, the person won't understand what you're talking about. Or your parent may even be offended! He or she may say, "What do you mean, forgive me? I haven't done anything wrong! I've always done the best I could."

Done the wrong way, saying you forgive a person can actually be an accusation. In other words, by saying, "I forgive you," you may in effect be saying, "You've done this terrible thing to me, but I'm going to overlook it." It's usually appropriate to say you forgive someone directly only if that person first approaches you, or in some other way makes it known that he realizes that he was in the wrong. He must in some way say, "I apologize." Then, the way will be paved for you to say, "I forgive you."

Even if a parent or anyone else hasn't reached the point where he realizes he must be forgiven, you can still approach him with a forgiving heart. Such an attitude will free *you* from inner resentment, which can play itself out in other relationships. You can say to yourself or to your confidant, "I know Mom and Dad did these particular things that hurt me, and I responded in a certain way to them, and together, those interactions are the source of my problem. But I don't hold anything against anybody. I forgive Mom and Dad for the things they did—and neglected to do. And if they ever indicate that they want me to, I'll tell them I forgive them right to their faces."

Such a forgiving attitude will do wonders to promote the healing process inside you. Most likely, you'll find that your feelings of anger, frustration, or resentment will begin to dissipate. You may find you are no longer doing things to get back at your parents or to avoid them. Moreover, you may find that your feelings and behavior with friends end up becoming more relaxed and positive than ever before.

As you can see, the process of "leaving" your parents—of resolving difficult emotional issues with them—is not designed to make you become an isolated, self-sufficient individual. Rather, the goal is to help you develop appropriate relationships with your parents and others. Our relationships with our parents are a vital and critical part of our lives, both as children and as adults. For this reason, those of us who are parents must always remember that we also have to resolve our relationships with *our* parents if we hope to develop positive, freeing, mature relationships with our own children.

## Step #2:
## Challenge Your Spouse to
## Become Your Partner

If you followed the suggestion in the previous chapter, the first move that you, as a parent, made to break the Dependent Love Pattern in your family was to find a confidant. If that confidant was your spouse, you have already begun working on this second step. You simply need to expand on it further by talking directly to your mate about needed improvements in your relationship.

On the other hand, if you did not feel able or comfortable confiding in your spouse initially, then you need to work a little harder to get him or her involved. First of all, you should realize that your overinvolvement is probably coupled with your spouse's underinvolvement. To correct that imbalance, you must challenge your husband or wife to become more involved, with both you and your children.

Since most often there is an overinvolved mother and an underinvolved father, I'm going to assume that this situation exists in the following discussion. If your situation is reversed, simply apply the illustrations in reverse.

At this point, you may object, "You just don't understand how difficult my husband is!" Or you may say, "Look, my husband does the best he can around the home. But after all, he's very busy with his work."

Actually, I do understand, but I find that many mothers I see underestimate themselves, their husbands, or their children. Devoted families are not weak, but rather, concerned and caring. You do have the strength to change this pattern and to get your husband more involved, once you realize how critical his participation is. Most likely, he actually does care more than you realize. The challenge is to find a way to tap that caring more effectively. By focusing first on your marriage, which is the central relationship in your family, you'll go a long way toward setting things right for both you and your children.

How can you challenge your husband to become involved?

First of all, you have to be more creative than you have been in the past in coming up with ways to involve your husband more with the family. Second, you may have to be more persistent in applying these new, innovative strategies.

You may think you've tried everything, but in fact there may be many creative ways left to approach your husband. In any event, as you begin to think of them, be sure to avoid blaming him, putting him down, or suggesting that you don't expect him to respond well to family problems. If you've tried blaming him or putting him down before, you undoubtedly know that this approach doesn't work very well.

A more productive tactic I've found is to let your husband know how important he is to the entire family. Tell him that you're really interested in hearing his perspective on what both of you should do to help the children. You might point out that you think you've underestimated what he can do in the family. For that matter, perhaps he's underestimated his own abilities. Invite him to join you—and let him know that you need his help. Certainly, there are things the children need that you, as the mother, cannot do, no matter how hard you try.

Speak to your husband in terms he can understand: point out the great emotional price of underinvolvement, and the valuable outcome of working together for change. Help him to see that his effort at becoming more involved is a great investment in a satisfying future family life. In short, it's essential that your family have two equal parents, not just a mother who does most of the child care and a father who stands in the background.

As you talk with your husband, be specific about what you think would help most with the children. Don't assume that he is going to be able to know automatically what to do. In fact, this child-rearing business may be quite new to him. You wouldn't assume that he already knows how to ski or ride a bicycle if he's never tried either sport before. So don't assume he's an expert in the even more difficult area of parenting.

As a first step, you might think of something you would most appreciate and that you are sure he is capable of doing. For example, one mother began by asking her husband to read the children their bedtime story on the two days when she worked. Another woman asked her husband to sit down with her to decide on a chore plan for the children. Whatever your husband is doing, simply ask for one small, specific step more. For some who see me for counseling, a first step may be asking the husband to join us for one counseling session.

In addition to being specific with your husband about what's needed, you'll need to encourage him as he tries to help. Let him know you appreciate the efforts he *is* making rather than harping on what he's not doing. Try to be thankful for each step he takes, no matter how small it may be. Remember that many small steps can produce major movement.

As he helps you work with the children, be aware that

his ideas are going to be different from yours. Don't approach him with preconceived notions and then expect him to follow them without any questions. For example, the husband I mentioned earlier agreed to read to the children—but not the stories his wife had planned for him to read. The other husband did help plan his children's chores, but his ideas for chores were a lot tougher than those his wife would have chosen. A real partnership assumes that *both* participants are going to contribute, both in the planning and in the execution stages.

What if your husband doesn't respond to this positive approach? In that case, you may need to explain to him how frustrated you're feeling and also exactly what your personal needs are. But again, don't offer these explanations while blaming him at the same time. For example, avoid a "you" approach: "You don't understand . . . you need to do this . . . you made a mistake doing that. . . ." With that kind of confrontational language, you'll most likely find him getting defensive. If that happens, any possibility of real communication may be destroyed.

So don't say, "You're never home for dinner on time! Not only that, you never get home at a reasonable hour so that you can help me with the children." Instead, using an "I" approach, you might tell him, "I really get frustrated when I have dinner ready and then you don't make it home in time. Also, I'm so tired by the end of the day that I'm overwhelmed trying to get the children ready for bed without help."

In other words, it's important to speak in terms of your own feelings, not his bad actions. It's easy for him to argue if you blame him, but it's very hard to argue if you explain your own personal feelings. After all, who knows your feelings better than you?

Another way to soften up a relatively unresponsive husband may be to start by admitting your own shortcomings and asking for his help in changing the whole situation. Here's an illustration: You might admit that in the past, you've tended to draw the children into conflicts with him. Or perhaps you've turned to them when you've had a problem, rather than to him.

To begin to correct such an imbalance, you might say, "You know, sometimes I avoid talking with you because I don't want to upset you. Sometimes I'm afraid I'll be unable to keep a cool head if you disagree with me." If you show him that you're vulnerable in this way, he'll be more likely to respond positively to help you overcome your weakness.

On the other hand, if your husband doesn't respond to any of these attempts, you may find that you have to be more challenging. You might have to let him know that if he doesn't help you actively with the children, you'll have to turn to other sources of support.

What might these "other sources of support" be? They'll be different for each family, but sometimes the answers might be a support group, such as Families Anonymous or Al-Anon. Or it may be a religious counselor, such as a pastor or rabbi. Or you might want to seek out a professional family therapist. In any case, by going to someone outside the family, you're letting your husband know that you mean business. You're saying that whether he helps or not, you're going to take steps to correct the problems that you perceive with the children.

In most cases, though, I find that a husband will respond positively at least to some degree without his wife taking drastic steps. A nurturing mother is often so afraid of causing bad feelings or "rocking the boat" that she wants to avoid conflict at any cost. As a result, she doesn't approach her husband to become her partner in dealing with family problems, even though he might be quite willing to participate if he were asked creatively and frankly.

In short, we frequently underestimate what husbands can do. Also, we often underestimate the power that wives and mothers have in initiating positive changes in their families. I can't count the number of times that a wife has told me, "I'll never get my husband to come in here for counseling." Yet she finds that when she asks him nicely, he does come. These unwilling husbands are usually upset by the family problems, too, and they want them resolved. It's just that they don't know how to go about it. They may feel uncomfortable admitting to outsiders that they have problems, and sometimes they feel they've never been invited to help search for solutions.

When a husband and wife are finally working together to change the situation in the family, it's important for them to work hard at that process of "cleaving," which we discussed earlier. Even as you learn to communicate with each other about your family's problems, be sure also to work at making time for fun together. This way, you can build on your strengths and develop your relationship as husband and wife.

What are some of the factors that will help you to "cleave" and work together as true partners during this phase? Here are a few things I've found helpful:

- Build on the positives in your relationship. For example, think of what you *do* like about each other and things you like doing together. Then, take time to enjoy those things. You might also consider building on your strengths by attending a communication course or enrichment seminar.
- Try to set aside a regular "date night," or time together for both fun and communication in a relaxing setting.
- When you do have a particular need or you feel a particular frustration with your husband, address him directly.
- Don't complain to others, or "hold in" your negative feelings about him. In a diplomatic way, get your gripes out on the table.
- Ask for your husband's presence regularly in family affairs, especially when you find yourself turning to your children to meet needs that your husband should fulfill.

- Bite your tongue when you find yourself pulling your children into a fight you're having with your husband.
- If you and your husband really seem to be at a dead end in some aspect of your relationship, or if you find yourselves getting into fights that destroy rather than build understanding, seek the help of a professional marriage therapist.

One of the most meaningful gifts you can give your children is your own good marriage. If you and your husband can indeed become genuine partners in the child-rearing experience, you'll find that your children are major beneficiaries, as they develop a balanced, loving relationship with both of you. Then, they'll be much more likely to become autonomous, effective adults, rather than adult children whose growth has been stunted.

At the same time, you and your husband will benefit as a couple. You'll find that as you learn to work together to raise your children, you can develop a relationship of great power and strength—a relationship that will carry you happily into your later years, after your children have grown up and gone off on their own. In a very real sense, the gift of a good marriage that you give to your children is an even bigger gift that you give to yourselves.

Up to this point we've focused on the interplay between husbands and wives. But what if you're a single parent? How can you get a "partner" if there's no spouse around to help you out?

One very helpful approach for single parents can be found in the next step, which deals with seeking outside support to enhance your inner strengths. But there's also another helpful strategy: to rely on the child's father, if he's alive, to assist you in whatever way he can.

Admittedly, it can be quite difficult, and perhaps even impossible, in some circumstances, to tap the resources of a divorced husband. You certainly don't want to trigger a new round of conflicts with your ex-spouse. Nor do you want to take a chance on catching your child in the middle of such battles.

On the other hand, every child does have two parents, with an important heritage from each of two families. Even if you want no relationship with your ex-spouse, he still will always be your child's father. So as painful as it may be, I would suggest that you encourage positive interactions, such as arranging for your child to visit his father as often as possible. Also, encourage the father to exercise his own visiting rights.

In addition, when you discuss the child's father at home, keep things positive. No doubt there are many bad things you could tell the child about his father, just as there are many bad things your ex-husband could—and possibly does—tell the child about you. But that's not the point. In most cases, there are also plenty of *good* things that each parent can communicate about the other. After all, you did choose each other to marry once upon a time: These are the messages that the child should hear.

In these ways, your youngster will develop a sense of belonging both to a father and a mother, even if he lives with only one parent. That sense of belonging and acceptance is extremely important in overcoming an excessive dependence on the parent who is doing most of the child care.

Many of these considerations also apply if your spouse is dead. Generally speaking, you probably won't have as many negative feelings about your deceased husband or wife. It should be a great deal easier to pass on positive information to your child. But what sometimes happens is that the dead parent is ignored, in the sense of never being referred to, and the surviving spouse may not keep in touch with the relatives on the other side of the child's family. Yet as in a divorce situation, it's important to give your youngster a sense of being linked to his other parent and family. In short, your youngster's identity shouldn't just be wrapped up in you, but should be broadened to include both parents as fully and positively as possible.

## Step #3:
## Seek Outside Support to Enhance
## Your Inner Strengths

If you're an overinvolved mother or father, you're certainly a person who tends to give totally of yourself. With such a giving nature, you also need to be replenished periodically by the nurturance and support of others. No matter how helpful your spouse may be as a partner, he or she can't be everything to you. If you expect your mate to fulfill all your needs, there's no doubt that he or she will fail you. Furthermore, if you're a single mother without a husband to help out, you'll need that outside support even more. So how do you get it?

At the outset, I think it's important to recognize the natural obstacles to finding such support. Most overinvolved parents do fail to seek this support for two main reasons:

First, it's often difficult for a family-oriented mother, who does everything for her children and her husband, to look outside the family for help. There's an assumption with such overinvolved parents that "people outside the family just aren't as trustworthy or understanding as those inside." The walls of family and blood in these families are often too high for many of these mothers to scale. If you feel this way, you must first recognize that "scaling that wall" is well worth the effort as an important way of redressing the imbalance in your family.

Second, you may object that with all of your other responsibilities, you don't have time to make additional friends or become involved in other activities. It may very well be true that your schedule is overloaded. What I'm talking about here is not just engaging in any other activity. You need to find a place where you *receive*, where you can share with others and gain help and advice as you are loved and understood.

To find time for this kind of nurturing support, you may very well have to give up some of your other commitments. I'm convinced that this kind of support is so important that it may be well worth your while to rearrange your schedule.

Still, where can you find this kind of support? Where can you receive emotional and spiritual help and get your "cup filled up" by helpful and understanding outsiders?

Sometimes, the source may be close friendships. To take advantage of these ties, you'll probably find you have to set up regular times to meet with your friends for coffee or lunches. You'll have to work at opening yourself up as well as listening in a way that makes these times provide real support. Other people may find that their most meaningful source of support is a prayer-and-share group at some church. Or there may be a parenting group or mothers' group at the local Y.

In any case, as you meet with these friends, you should feel secure that the things you share with them will be held in confidence. In other words, you don't want your deepest concerns about your spouse and your family to be spread all over the neighborhood immediately after you leave your friends' presence.

For those families confronting problems with alcohol or drugs, support groups like Al-Anon or ACOA (Adult Children of Alcoholics) are essential. The particular difficulties of dealing with alcohol and drugs make these groups especially helpful because those who participate have had considerable experience with the same problem you're facing.

In short, you've probably become overinvolved with your children because you seek and need a great deal of personal closeness with other people. There's certainly nothing wrong with needing intimacy with others, but it's important to learn to fill this need in a way that is healthier for both you and your children. Specifically, you should establish ties with concerned and sensitive people outside your family, as well as with your mate. It's only with such support that you can hope to be fully successful in the remaining steps in this sequence.

## Step #4: Give Your Children Wings

As you already know, emotionally healthy children need not only strong "roots" but also strong wings. By definition, the roots of acceptance, love, and nurturance are usually there in devoted families, even where the mother has become overinvolved and the father remains emotionally distant. But too often, independence and confidence are missing, or they are so stunted that the child finds himself struggling in his adult life against the downward pull of dependence.

How can dependent children from devoted families grow?

The basic principle in helping a child develop independence and confidence is to do it one step at a time. In other words, begin from where the child is in his development, and move out gradually from there. Don't expect huge changes all at once. Instead, look for little steps, which can build the child up gradually over a period of time. As the child changes and grows, praise him for the progress he's making, no matter how small it may be.

For example, if you have a preschool son who sleeps regularly with you every night, you don't want to change things drastically by saying, "Okay, you have to sleep by yourself from now on. You'll be in your own bed, all night, every night!"

Instead, you might start by being sure that your son has his own "big boy" bed in his own room, a bed that is both inviting and comfortable for him. Among other things, you might see that he has colorful, interesting sheets and bedspreads, along with plenty of soft, fuzzy toy animals.

After you have the physical setup in place, let your son know ahead of time that you're expecting him to start sleeping by himself. To ease the process, you might lie down with him in his bed or sit by his bed until he falls asleep. If he wakes up during the night at first, you might lead him back into bed and then sit with him until he falls back to sleep again.

Each time he inches forward, no matter how slightly, you should praise him. Don't point out how far he has to go, or say he should be growing more quickly than he is.

Gradually, you should try to stay with your son for shorter and shorter periods of time until finally, he can make it through the entire night on his own. In other words, don't try to get the child to break a deeply ingrained habit all at once, in one day. Rather, help him over a period of time until he can do the full task with a real feeling of accomplishment.

The same principles apply with teenagers. If you have a teenage daughter who does almost no chores around the house, you can't expect to change her overnight. You may have gotten into the habit of doing all the cooking, cleaning, and other housework. In that case, you can't expect to put everything on her shoulders, with little warning or without preparing her for the task. In fact, she may not know how to do certain jobs, or what standards are expected of her.

You might begin by saying, "I know how well you do this or that. But I also know that you could do a number of other things around the house here, if you had the chance. It's just that we haven't given you the opportunity or helped you to learn. So, let's talk a little about what you might be able to do to increase your responsibilities around the house—what you'd prefer to do and what you'd rather not do. At the same time, we might even discuss what you would like for us to do for you."

In discussions like this, it's helpful if both the father and mother participate with the child. That way, the parents present a solid front. Then, when an agreement is reached, it's clear that everyone has assented to it. Furthermore, by approaching a problem in this way—where there's the possibility of some give-and-take on the part of both parents and children—the idea of doing more around the house may become more interesting to your daughter. She'll see that by taking on extra responsibilities, she may also receive certain benefits in return. As with younger children, it will be helpful if you start your teenager with small tasks and work up to more difficult ones.

The girl we've been considering, for instance, might indicate that she wants to help with preparing the meals. So she might begin with preparing the salad for dinner once a week, with no cooking responsibilities at all. Next, after a certain period of time, she might move on to cooking one part of the dinner each evening. Then, she might do one entire meal once a week.

As your child learns a new task, there are at least two different approaches to take. On the one hand, the youngster can do the entire job, and you can give a considerable amount of help at the beginning. Then, you can gradually lessen your help until your child is doing the entire task by herself. On the other hand, you can have the child do one small step in a larger task completely by herself. When she has that under control, you can add one more step until she's doing the entire job.

Obviously, there's no set formula for any of these approaches. You'll just have to examine each task and responsibility as it comes up and see what will work best. In general, the "best" is whatever is most likely to ensure success for the child. If the child bravely takes on a new thing and fails miserably at it, it's going to be hard to get her to try again. So give as much help as it takes. Teach carefully, and don't assume your child knows how to do something just because it seems simple and obvious to you. Take your time.

As you're helping your child to grow, I find it helpful to keep several practical considerations in mind:

- Always look for new learning opportunities for your child. When you give her the opportunity, don't take it back from her and try to do it better. Let her struggle through it, with your encouragement, until she can do the job herself.

- Identify those tasks that require instruction, and plan to teach and act as a guide along the way. In this case, you're not taking the task over from the child but getting involved in helping her learn difficult skills that she lacks.
- When you set definite household tasks or responsibilities for a child, be sure to agree on consequences: In other words, try to include positive privileges or rewards when the job is done properly, as well as negative outcomes if the job isn't done right. Be sure to follow through with your consequences. If you don't, you'll lose all credibility and be back to nagging and complaining, rather than seeing your child take on and fulfill new responsibilities.
- Listen to your child as she tries to exercise her new responsibilities. If she complains, don't say, "Oh you can do it!" or, "Quit bellyaching and get on with it!" without listening fully. Your child may be telling you something important. Maybe the task needs some adjusting to fit her age and ability levels. Or maybe she just needs extra encouragement.
- Encourage your child to get involved with outside friends and activities. In most enmeshed devoted families, where the child has developed an unhealthy dependence on one or both parents, the youngster often lacks social skills. If your child has had few outside experiences with others and has developed few social skills, when she gets off on her own, she's much more likely to make serious mistakes. On the other hand, if you encourage your child to get involved in peer activities, she's much more likely to develop the social skills she needs. She'll then be in a better position to make wiser decisions as she gets older.
- Believe in your child. Spend some time identifying your child's talents and interests, and then tell your youngster what they are and encourage her to develop these strengths. Make it clear that there are lots of things she can do, rather than focus on the

things that she can't do. Find activities and challenges that you know your youngster can succeed at. Then, put her in a position where she's likely to do well rather than fail.

Even when you're dealing with your child's negative traits, try to see a positive side to those characteristics, and then encourage the positive. For example, what seems to be laziness or a failure to pay attention to the task at hand may actually reflect a peculiar kind of thoughtfulness or creative fantasy. Or talking too much could be having a way with words. Rudeness could be self-assuredness. Shyness, or a reluctance to speak out in conversations, could also mean that a child is potentially a good listener. If you emphasize the positive, even as you're dealing with the negative, your child is much more likely to become convinced that you really believe in her. If you believe in your youngster and let her know that, you can be sure that she'll begin to believe in herself.

## Step #5: Take a Vacation

Many times, when a Dependent Love Pattern begins to wreak havoc in a loving home, it's necessary for the overinvolved parent, often the mother, to "take a vacation." What exactly do I mean by this? The main idea is to take a physical and emotional break from doing so much for your children or for your spouse. As it happens, some mothers have taken quite an extreme approach to this sort of vacationing.

One mother of a forty-five-year-old perpetual child finally decided that the only way she was going to escape her parenting duties—and help her son break his dependency pattern—was literally to leave her home. Her son slept on her sofa all day, came in and out of the house whenever he felt like it, and never contributed to the household income or responsibilities. So, every so often, when she was totally burned out, she would close up her home completely and actually leave the country for a few weeks or even months.

Another mother, a sixty-year-old overinvolved parent, actually began to consider selling her house and buying a condominium. She knew the new place would be too small to house her three dependent children, all in their thirties, who were still living with her.

As I say, these are extreme examples, and I certainly don't suggest that you go as far as these two rather tortured mothers. There are other ways of "taking a vacation" before you get to the point of having to leave the country or sell your home!

The main idea is to encourage your children toward greater responsibility and independence by setting specific limits on what you'll do for them. In effect, you're deciding that you've worked long and hard all your life as a mother and homemaker, and now you deserve a vacation. It's time for you to stop doing only for others and start doing more for yourself. At the same time, you should realize that as you stop doing as much for your children, you're really, in fact, doing *more* for them—because you're helping them to become competent adults in their own right.

Specifically, how do you go about taking such a vacation? As I see it, there are three main stages.

*First stage.* Decide on the kind of vacation you need to take. To make this decision, you might begin by focusing on the things that frustrate you most around the home. What do you usually argue with your children about? What responsibilities do you take on for them that they should be doing for themselves? To jog your memory, consider a few illustrative examples.

You have a ten-year-old, a thirteen-year-old, and a husband, all of whom like to eat different things. You've slipped into the position of cooking nine meals a day. You might take a vacation by deciding, "I'm only going to cook three meals a day, and anyone who wants something different will have to get it himself!"

You're frustrated with trying to get your children to pick up their clothes and put them in the clothes hamper. You take a vacation by saying once, quite clearly, "I'll only wash what's in the hamper on Tuesdays and Fridays—and I'm not going to wash anything that's not in the hamper." If your youngsters run out of underwear or other attire a couple of times, they'll start remembering to put the clothes in the hamper where they should be.

You've become "Mom's Taxi Service" because you find yourself running back and forth getting things that the children have forgotten to take to various activities. You decide to make only a limited number of "taxi runs" each day for each week, and you tell your children exactly what those trips will be. Then, the children will have to take on the responsibility of remembering for themselves the lunch box or book that they always tend to forget. If they want a ride to another place, they'll have to make other arrangements.

You feel like a human alarm clock because somehow it's become your responsibility to be sure that everyone gets up in the morning. You decide to take a vacation by giving each child and your spouse his own alarm clock. You no longer make sure the others are up and off in the mornings. After people have overslept a couple of times, you'll probably have no further problems, and everyone will have become more responsible for his own affairs.

As you can see, when you decide on the kind of "vacation" you're going to take, you have to be specific. It's important to be precise about *what* responsibilities you're going to give up, *when* you're going to give them up, and *how* you're going to give them up.

Also, be sure to begin with something that you're certain you can follow through on. Don't pick a "vacation" that will be too hard for you. Remember: If you can't follow through on your decision, you'll be right back where you started, doing too much for others and probably complaining even more about your frustrations.

\* \* \*

*Second stage.* Next, after you've decided on the kind of vacation you're going to take, you should announce firmly and clearly to all the concerned parties just what you're going to do so they can plan for it. Just stopping certain things without warning may cause undue confusion on the part of other family members, and they may put additional pressure on you to revert to your old ways.

On the other hand, it won't help to make this announcement if you don't follow up on it. In fact, if you fail to act after your announcement, your family may believe you're just engaging in hollow threats or nagging, which they will feel free to ignore.

*Third stage.* Actually take the vacation!

You can be sure that taking a break from your family responsibilities will meet with many of the same obstacles that you face when you get ready for a real vacation with your family. In other words, someone always gets sick, special needs arise, or unexpected work intervenes.

You should stick to your resolve, regardless of your own guilt feelings or your children's complaints. Your sons, your daughters, and your spouse know better than anyone how to play your heartstrings in order to keep you from taking this new course of action. So brace yourself and plan for the worst possible scenario. Then, sit back and enjoy yourself as you find you really don't have to carry all those unnecessary family burdens on your shoulders.

## Step 6: Try Growing

Let's assume now you're a *former* overinvolved parent, who has succeeded with the first five steps in this sequence. You should find that you and your family are largely free from the Dependent Love Pattern that has shackled your children and robbed them of their independence. But you're also in a position that's rather unusual for you. Since you have a lot of free time on your hands because your youngsters are more independent and more equipped to handle responsibilities on their own, it's quite likely that you feel a certain emptiness and even loneliness in your life.

When you've cared so much for your children for so long, and then no longer have them around to receive your attention and concern, you may end up feeling miserable. That's why spouses should work together as full partners in dealing with family problems. If you've worked at developing your marriage in this way, you'll find that you have a solid source of support and nurturance that can help to fill the void you may feel in the absence of your children.

Even with the presence of a supportive mate, you'll most likely find that you need other ways to occupy your time, other ways to "fly." This may involve getting a job or volunteering in some worthwhile activity. Perhaps you'd like to focus on some sort of work that dovetails with your past tasks and interests, such as helping out in a day care center or starting a catering business. Or you may want to get more involved in your local church or synagogue.

In any case, as a naturally nurturing and loving person, you'll need to find outlets for your interests and needs, now that your children are learning to grow on their own. You've pretty much completed one job well, so apply for some new jobs or at least find enjoyable activities for "retirement" from parenting.

You need to let yourself grow in ways that you may never have anticipated. Now is the time to make some of those old dreams of yours come true. Also, take a chance to dream some new dreams—and feel the exhilarating freedom that comes from reaching new heights of achievement and satisfaction.

# Chapter 13

# ADULT CHILDREN *CAN* GROW WINGS!

I'm constantly hearing people express the same aspirations in my counseling sessions: "I want to take charge of my life . . . I want some control over my future . . . Too many people are telling me what to do! . . . I've got to break free of my parents and start living my own life."

The greatest challenge for adult children who have grown up in loving but over-caring homes is to break free of the Dependent Love Pattern that may be preventing them from developing their full potential. They will then be in a position to grow the independence and competence that are necessary for maximum success and satisfaction in life. And believe me, you *can* grow! No matter how dependent you have become on your parents, you can still learn the skills and develop the self-confidence you need to reach your personal potential.

To achieve this goal, you first must learn to "leave" home. Most likely, you're too closely tied to your mother; you lack a deep relationship with your father; and you don't have enough deep, sharing peer relationships and friendships. The process of "leaving" involves adjusting all these relationships so that they're in better balance. You should move toward:

- less dependence on your mother;
- more involvement with your father; and
- greater closeness with your peers.

Your objective should be mature adult interactions in each relationship.

Leaving home gracefully can be difficult when you come from a devoted family. Many children with over-involved parents feel that the only way to become independent is to cut off their relationships with Mom and Dad completely. Some run away from home; others provoke a big blow-up and walk out in a huff. Still others just try to avoid any further contact by moving miles away from home.

Usually, though, such radical steps leave children still enmeshed with their parents, because they carry with them all the negative baggage of unresolved relationships. This baggage may cause them to deal with their own children, spouse, or friends in an unbalanced manner, such as by becoming too involved or controlling with them, or not involved enough.

A much better way to ''leave'' parents is to stop playing a childish role with them. Your ultimate goal should be *appropriate*, adult-to-adult relationships with them. A mature adult relationship with each of your parents will mean that you:

- speak up for yourself and your spouse;
- have your own opinions and express them;
- disagree openly when necessary, without blowing up;
- disregard unreasonable family rules when they conflict with your own rules or values; and
- show a caring concern for your parents without conforming to their standards of overinvolvement.

To become more of an independent adult with your parents, I've found that it's very helpful to observe certain rules or guidelines that can help you develop the independence that you now lack. As we go through each of these six rules, always keep in mind this underlying objective: Your goal in "leaving" your parents is not to cut off relationships with them, but to correct any imbalance in the relation. Specifically, you want to break free of the excessive control exercised by the smothering parent and to develop new lines of communication and love with the more distant parent.

### Rule #1:
### Stop Being Dependent on
### Your Smothering Parents

The first step is to learn to say no to offers of help from your smothering mother or father. As you know, children from enmeshed devoted families grow used to having things done for them. While it's natural for preschool kids to be the recipients of a lot of parental help, in the case of an older child this kind of help does more harm than good.

As you embark on this course, you may find yourself confronted with mixed emotions. You want to break free, but you feel bad about pulling away. As you've grown older, you've probably begun to detest the idea of always being treated like a child or required to be always available when in fact you're an adult. Yet the hate you feel for this role will be countered by the love you feel for Mom and your secret worries about what she will do without you to care for. If you're the youngest, the burden on you may seem even greater because your departure will be the final act that creates the "empty nest" for Mom.

You may be acutely aware that because of your dependent relationship in your family, you have become your mother's main job. If your dad tends to be emotionally distant from the rest of the family, you may be providing your mother with her main source of moral support and companionship. Without you, she may suddenly find herself isolated and alone, with no one to talk to or confide in.

As the sensitive child of loving parents, you probably realize what a critical role you play in your family. As a result, you may be reluctant to give up this role because you want to keep your mother and father happy. After all, Mom says she *likes* to do your cooking and laundry. These activities do keep her busy and put the two of you in constant contact.

You may have become your mother's main purpose in life because you created problems for her throughout your life. Maybe you've gotten into trouble at school or with the law. Or perhaps you have special physical or emotional needs that take up a great deal of her time.

But remember: You have been playing a role that you can *never* successfully fulfill. Your father has been emotionally distant from your mother, and that created the initial vacuum in her life that you stepped in to fill. That vacuum really needs to be filled by your father or another peer of your mother's. You need to step back and allow that vacuum in your mother's life to return so that the way will be cleared for a more appropriate person to enter.

You face a difficult and often painful decision. When you choose not to sacrifice your life in order to give your mother a job and companion, you will probably produce an uncomfortable situation for your parents. But without that discomfort, neither you nor your parents can move forward to the next stage of family growth or to activities and relationships that will ultimately be more rewarding.

As you go through this process of separating from your overinvolved mother, your feelings are likely to alternate between intense love and concern on the one hand, and resentment and even hate on the other. One young woman whom I saw on a regular basis would have destructive,

angry outbursts at her mother on certain occasions, curs-
ing, throwing objects, and adamantly refusing to do anything that she was asked to do. Yet afterward, this
daughter would worry about her mother's welfare and
check up on her dutifully.

What this young woman didn't realize was that her
very loving devotion and dependency on her mother,
which lacked any appropriate limits, laid the groundwork
for later outbursts of intense anger and the frustrated
feeling of being trapped. Such a love–hate reaction is
almost inevitable unless you decide to become independent of Mom and take steps to start living your own life.

To "cut the apron strings," it's often necessary for the
adult child to decide, in effect, "This has gone far
enough! Time for a change!" But before you can say "no
thanks" to a smothering parent lovingly and effectively,
it's necessary to think through the typical situation that
you expect to encounter and to plan new ways to respond.

For example, you may know that your mother waits on
you hand and foot when you visit her. So think through
each situation—your laundry, meals, various errands or
whatever other tasks she performs for you. Then consider
carefully how you can politely and graciously—but firmly
and clearly—say, "No thanks, I'd really rather do that
myself and give you a break."

As you think through your relationship with Mom or
Dad, try to anticipate the objections she or he is likely
to raise as you move to break the dependency pattern. Be
prepared for all the logical—and the illogical—reasons
your parent may give you for continuing with the excessive help and overinvolvement in your life.

You've surely heard many of them before: "You know
you don't know how to do your own laundry!" Or, "No
need for you to get up when I'm already up." Or, "You
know you don't have time to wash your own clothes all
the time—and I'm *happy* to do it!"

Or your parent may just agree with you and then go

right on "helping" you despite your request. Expect these responses so that instead of becoming angry, you will have a next step ready. Remember, you're dealing with habits and patterns that have taken years to develop. Don't expect to transform an entire relationship overnight, but do plan and determine to take small but significant steps that will ultimately improve your relationship.

As you plan your "escape," be prepared to wrestle with your own inclination toward comfort, as well as your tendency to give in when Mom insists on helping you. You may catch yourself thinking, "Well, maybe she's got a point. It really is easier and more convenient for me just to let her do it." Yet even as these thoughts come into your mind, look at the bigger picture. Remember the personal costs that you may be paying by continuing to be dependent on her. Then, plan some way to overcome your own inertia, as well as the resistances you meet from Mom and Dad.

Of course, what I'm presenting here is a worst-case scenario. You may expect resistance from your parents only to find that Mom and Dad are quite grateful and relieved at your offer to take over more responsibilities. After all, your mother and father are growing older, and the chances are, they've been looking forward to greater freedom now that you've become an adult. Yet your mother may feel that to be a "good mother," she needs to continue doing for you until you explicitly release her from this responsibility.

What are some other practical steps you can take to assert your independence and separate yourself from Mom? In addition to this basic approach, here are a few other tips for saying "no thanks" when it seems she may try to do too much for you.

Show her that you can do things by yourself by taking the initiative away from her. You might do your own laundry rather than waiting for her to do it. Or you might get up and get your own snacks for your television viewing, rather than allowing her to wait on you hand and foot.

Reduce the extent to which you act as your mother's confidant. This doesn't mean that you should stop talking with her sensitively and lovingly. But instead of listening to her complaints about Dad or asking for her advice, talk more about your respective activities and goals, and also your mutual relationships.

Feel free to disagree with her and stand up for your own opinions in her presence, but do this calmly and firmly, like an adult. When a dependent adult child allows a smothering relationship with his mother to continue for a long period of time, he may be inclined to explode, like a pent-up volcano. By disagreeing in a low-key way when you first sense a conflict, you'll be less likely to explode internally or externally later on.

Begin to define your life and activities not simply in relationship to your mother's needs and schedule, but in terms of your own schedule.

Admit that you simply can't do everything that your Mom wants you to do. You might say, "I'm really sorry, Mom, but I'm very busy with my own responsibilities and my own family. I just don't have time to be with you as much as I have in the past." Such statements can be painful, and you should be prepared to see your mother look hurt and perhaps even shed some tears. But this pain is well worth the reward of a more mature and enjoyable relationship.

Take some concrete steps to help your mother develop emotional support from people other than yourself. You might get in contact with your own sisters and brothers, some of her friends, or members of her church or synagogue. Encourage them to reach out more to her during this time of transition. Encourage your father to do more with her as well. The more you can talk to him frankly about the Dependent Love Pattern that has developed in your family—without blaming him or getting too "psychological'' in your discussions—the more likely he will be to respond positively in filling the vacuum that you've left.

If you're married, focus clearly on what your main priorities in life should be with your own family. There's no doubt that your own spouse and children must come before any relationship you have with your mother and father. If you're going to give such a priority to your own family, you'll have to give them the lion's share of your time and energy each day.

When you have an argument with your spouse, don't call either of your parents to seek advice. Work out the disagreement with your husband or wife, even if that is difficult with only the two of you involved.

When you have a choice as to whom you should be with at a particular time or whose opinion you should follow on a particular issue, pick your partner over your parents. Showing this kind of loyalty and support to your spouse will help strengthen your own marriage and facilitate the process of separation from your parents.

### Rule #2:
### Get Closer to Your
### Emotionally Distant Parent

Your smothering, overloving mother is probably paired with an emotionally distant father. To promote a better balance in your family relationships, you shouldn't just focus on Mom. It's also important to reach out to Dad and try to develop a closer relationship and better lines of communication with him. As you grow closer to your father, you'll find that you spend more time with him and pull back from that unhealthy overinvolvement with your mother.

I don't want to give the impression that this change is easy. On the contrary, it may be quite difficult to get closer to Dad because he may always have been more difficult to speak to, or because he may have been less available to you and other family members.

Any moves that you make toward him may threaten your mother. She may sense immediately that she's in danger of no longer having you exclusively to herself. In short, as with many of the other major challenges in our lives, being forewarned is being forearmed, as you begin the seemingly innocent process of trying to build a close relationship with your father.

In my counseling, I've discovered a number of helpful strategies that can make this effort to get closer to your father a little easier.

*Phone conversations.* Many children tell me that when they get a phone call from their parents, the mother usually places the call. Then, the father may get on the phone for a perfunctory few seconds, and before you know it, he's off. Or if the child calls home and the father answers, he'll often just say, "Well, how're you doing? Hold on just a minute and I'll get your mother." Then, he'll immediately yell for her and that's the last you'll hear from him.

What can you do to change these situations? One approach is to pick a time to call when you know that only your father will be home. Of, if both parents are at home, prepare some questions or conversational tidbits for him ahead of time, and keep him on the phone with you as long as possible. The more accustomed he gets to talking with you, the more likely he will be to communicate at greater length in future conversations.

If you call home and your mother answers the telephone, be ready with a special message for your father and, if possible, make that the main purpose for your call. Ask specifically for him and then talk with him about what you've planned to say.

*Visits to parents.* When you visit your parents, you may find that your mother seeks you out for conversations, while your father tends to avoid you. He may stay away from you and your mother when the two of you get involved in personal communications. Prepare ahead of time in your telephone conversations to engage him in discussions of certain topics that you know he'll be interested in or that will help you gain understanding.

You can request your father's company for a joint activity, just for the two of you. If he likes to fish, tell him you want him to take you out some morning. Or if he enjoys some activity or is available for lunch some day, try to arrange a special get-together.

In your first efforts to reach out to your father, be satisfied with short conversations and encounters. Again, it's those little steps that can lead you in a productive direction over a period of weeks and even months. You don't have to have a heavy conversation with him and try to resolve all the problems in your relationship in one sitting.

It will be helpful for you to draw him out with specific questions that might be rather impersonal at first. Then, begin to delve more deeply into his feelings and your relationship. You might get him to tell you something about his childhood and family background. Most parents enjoy telling their children about their mother, father, and siblings and trying to piece together the various factors that made them into the persons that they now are. After you've laid the groundwork with these non-threatening questions, you might get more personal about your father's feelings and at the same time reveal some of your own emotions and struggles.

Eventually, you may want to have a rather long, frank conversation with your father to tell him how you've missed having a closer relationship with him and hope for his advice and support now. Confide in him about a specific problem you're struggling with in your effort to become more competent. For example, you might pose issues like being on time, developing positive relationships with men, or fixing things in your apartment.

Before you engage in such a discussion, it's important to think over what his possible responses may be and how you'll reply. For example, he might just nod his head and say nothing as you explain your position to him. Or he might become angry. Or he might tell your mother, and she might get mad and feel betrayed. Think about how you can respond well to his reactions. Be prepared for the worst! Remember that he is not likely to change, at least not quickly. But by changing your approach, the relationship will change. Usually, I've found that when people are prepared for the worst, they are pleasantly surprised when something less serious happens than they anticipate.

As you reach out to your father in these ways, you may very well find that the greatest opposition you face comes from your mother. One young man whom I was counseling had homosexual inclinations, which he said made him feel uncomfortable. Although he wanted to talk to his dad about this matter, he felt very limited in what he could say because of his mother. She had insisted that she be the only one in the family to know about his problem. As she said, "I want to spare the others—and especially your father—from any hurt."

Instead of sparing any hurt, her attitude, and her son's acquiescence in it, had created a greater distance and discomfort in the other family relationships. The father and son had even less to say to each other than in the past. Meanwhile, the unnatural, overinvolved bond between mother and son had intensified.

How did this young man break free of this dependency connection? The most powerful and effective step he took was to disregard his mother's advice, go to his father, and tell him that he had homosexual inclinations. He said he was in the process of trying to deal with his problem, but needed his dad's help. With that communication, the mother's "spell" over her son—including her tendency to become overinvolved with him—was broken. At the same time, the father, instead of being "hurt," was concerned and helpful toward his son. As a result, father and son developed a much closer relationship than they had ever experienced before.

These are just a few ways that fathers and children can grow closer together and put their family relationships in better balance. The most important point underlying any advice or practical strategies is this: Don't sell your dad short! Don't underestimate his ability to enter into a close, loving relationship with you, even if he's been extremely distant and even neglectful in the past. Distant fathers, like dependent children, often don't like the role that they've fallen into, but they don't know how to escape it. With the help of other family members, a distant dad can contribute to helping the entire family break free of the Dependent Love Pattern.

## Rule #3:
## Give Up the Mediator Role
## Between Your Parents

This third rule reminds me of the ropes that keep a hot-air balloon lashed to the ground. Those lines have to be untied or cut for the balloon to soar up into the air. Similarly, if you have stumbled into the role of mediator in your parents' marriage, both your mother and your father may be holding you down with emotional "ropes." Sometimes the interactions may be so subtle that children—and that includes adult children—may be completely unaware that they've assumed the role of mediators.

I'm reminded of one family where the mother and father would disagree on some subject. Then, each would approach the child and "unload" his or her arguments on the youngster in an effort to get an extra "vote" or moral support for his or her particular position.

Typically, the issues that the parents would approach the son about would be those in which they knew his opinion could have an impact. Even when he was small, for example, the boy might say adamantly that he didn't want to go on a certain vacation. In such a case, his opinion plus the opinion of one of the parents would always carry the day. If the mother didn't want to take a trip to a spot that her husband was promoting, she might clandestinely mention all the negative aspects of the place to her son. Using such tactics, she would turn him against the father's suggestions. The boy's negative attitude would then make it certain that Dad would lose.

This pattern of conduct continued even after the boy grew into adulthood—until he finally realized what was going on. In order to break free of his mediating role, where he was subtly locked into the conflicts between the parents, he decided first of all just not to talk to his mother about his father, or to his father about his mother. He refused to console his mother about his father, or commiserate with his father about his mother.

If he was approached by either parent on a touchy subject, the son would be very direct in his response: "I really would rather not get into that, Mom," he might say. Or he might respond, "Dad, I really think that's something between you and Mom. I'm sure you can handle it. I really don't see that I can have much input in it."

In this way, he forced his parents to deal with each other directly, rather than deal with him as their mediator.

As with the other rules, it will be necessary for you, as the concerned child, to think clearly and specifically about the typical family conversations and patterns that you face. Then, prepare a specific strategy to deal with the pressures that your mother or father is likely to put on you. Many times, it's advisable to practice responses with your confidant before you actually try them with your parents. In some cases, I've found it helpful for people with this problem to write out their strategies and even the responses that they expect to make to their parents.

## Rule #4:
## Be Your Real Self Around Your Family

Too often, children who come from devoted families develop two personalities—one for Mom and Dad, and one for everybody else.

Suppose when you become an adult that you move away from home and begin your own life. Among other things, you decide to start your own family, and you develop in ways that may be quite different from your childhood behaviors and beliefs. For example, if you're planning to get married, you may choose your prospective mate for reasons that your parents might not understand or even approve of. Or you may have decided to affirm a new religious faith or be planning a career change.

Whatever you're doing out there in the real world as an adult, you may hesitate to share your thoughts or decisions with your parents because you may worry that they won't approve. When you return home for a visit or lengthy stay, you'll probably find youself reverting to childhood patterns and behaviors in a variety of ways. I've seen many young women and men who acted like completely mature, rational adults when they were around their peers or pursuing their occupations. But when they went back home for a visit with Mom and Dad, they would immediately revert to childish ways.

One young man, a rather successful lawyer, started falling back into an almost-quasi-whining attitude around his mother as he resisted her attempts to get him to help out with some chores around the house. As it happened, she had pushed him and nagged him to assume responsibilities like this all his life. But she had never followed through on her requests, and he had always managed to get out of work by saying, "Aw, ma, I just don't feel like it right now. How about a little later, okay?"

Similarly, a grown-up daughter had recently married and had stopped off to visit "the folks" on a cross-country car trip. She almost immediately got into a nasty argument with her mother because Mom started making negative comments about the daughter's choice of clothing.

Another young woman had undergone a dramatic religious conversion experience, but she avoided telling her parents about it for more than a year because she was afraid that they would laugh at her or try to talk her out of "that kind of fanaticism."

Each of these cases, though different, contains a common thread—a tendency to be one person in the presence of your parents and a different person with other people. In order to become a truly independent adult and to escape the Dependent Love Pattern of your background, it's necessary to become *one* person for *everybody*. After all, you've already made certain decisions as an adult. Those decisions give you a status of independence and a special identity that differentiates you from your parents and everyone else. To be sure, you still have strong links with your parents and the rest of your family. At the same time, you are your own person. It's important for you to celebrate your individual uniqueness in their presence, as well as outside their presence.

If you are direct and honest with your parents, you'll probably find they're much more understanding and accepting than you anticipated they would be. Even if they're not, it's important to let them know where you stand so you can continue to move on in the maturing process. Most of the time, parents prefer that approach to just cutting them off.

If you are married, becoming the same person with your parents and with your spouse is especially important. For one thing, you owe it to your husband or wife to stand up for him or her and to be an adult in your joint dealings with your mom and dad. If you usually revert to childhood when you go home, you'll be sorely tempted to side with your parents or let them control any interactions that may involve your spouse. Such an attitude can be extremely dangerous to your marriage because you'll in effect be saying to your husband or wife, "I'm sorry, dear, but when we're around Mom and Dad, we have to do as they say."

Furthermore, if you revert to childhood around your parents in the presence of your spouse and your children, your kids are likely to become, in effect, the children of your parents. Whatever rules you may have established at home about your youngsters' conduct will disintegrate as your parents begin to impose their rules on your children.

It's much better—if you happen to be a mother with a smothering mother, for example—to respond to your mother's overinvolvement like this:

- follow your own best judgment in deciding how often to see your parents or have your children see their grandparents;
- thank your mother for her concern and advice, but let her know you are an adult and able to operate quite well as a parent;
- ask your mother to share fewer of her ideas so you can learn to be a parent on your own;
- tell your mother—who is now a grandmother—that it's time for her to relax and take a vacation from the responsibilities and worries of parenting;
- make your rules clear and firm, and confront your mother if she contradicts or breaks them with your children;
- in the most serious cases, explain that because your child needs continuity, you'll have to bring your children over less often if your rules aren't kept; and
- thank your mother for her willingness to help, but politely yet firmly decline her help when it gets in the way of your own role as parent.

I realize that all of this may sound quite complicated, and in fact, it can become complicated. To avoid excessive complexity, aim to be your one *real* self in the presence of your mother and father—as well as the outside world. Everything becomes so much simpler if you play it straight with Mom and Dad. Just let them know who you really are, and then proceed to live your own adult life. Put your priorities in proper order, with your own spouse and kids getting top billing in your life. Then, your relationship with your mother and father can move into a healthier, more balanced position in your total family picture.

## Rule #5:
## Build Genuine Peer Friendships

In many devoted families—and especially those with an overinvolved parent, such as a smothering mother—there may be a tendency for family members to establish really close relationships only with those in the family. Certainly, the warm, outgoing personalities that are often developed in devoted families make it easy for members to establish many cordial outside acquaintances. But often, these friendships are not really close.

To test your friendships, just to see how close they are, try asking yourself these questions:

- Do you confide your inner hurts and frustrations to your friends?
- Which friends do you speak with more regularly than with your mother?
- Which friends have you been able to fight with and disagree with—and yet emerge on the other side of the argument with a stronger, deeper relationship?

Usually, an ability to communicate and relate on these levels is limited to the deepest, most authentic kinds of friendships. Such intimacy is not possible with passing acquaintances, or even with those whom most of us would really regard as "friends." In short, there's a tendency among devoted family members to limit the deepest personal relationships to those within the family rather than to encompass outsiders.

In fact, a major characteristic of enmeshed, unbalanced loving families, where dependency relationships prevail, is that family members refuse to let outsiders into the intimate circle. Being able to reach out and begin to develop peer friendships on the deepest levels is one of the final steps in breaking free from the Dependent Love Pattern within a family.

How can outside friends help? One of the reasons that members of devoted families resist bringing outsiders into their confidence is that the family members fear that the outsiders will see family faults and may reject them or fail to understand the family's real problems. Actually, these outsiders—if they are truly perceptive and caring people—can give us an objective picture of ourselves. They can help us see ourselves in perspective, laugh at our idiosyncrasies, and glimpse new possibilities for relationships. Furthermore, they can often provide the support we need to break free of the dependencies that are holding us back from our full potential.

As you reach out and try to establish intimate relationships with outsiders, it's important to be careful of one peculiar danger. Sometimes, when people from enmeshed devoted families enter into certain marriages or friendships, they may become very intimate with other people. Yet their intimacy may be just recreating the unhealthy, smothering, dependent patterns that characterized their original families.

I've encountered a number of young men, for instance, who came out of families with overinvolved mothers. Then, each proceeded to marry a domineering, overinvolved wife who did everything for him, just as his mother was in the habit of doing.

In a similar vein, a young woman, who came out of a family with a smothering mother and an emotionally distant father, moved far away from her parents and began an independent career as an adult. Still, the influence of her family stuck with her. She was always attaching herself to one or two people, whom she regarded as "best friends." Yet these friends, in effect, became a smothering, overinvolved mother substitute for her in her new life. She would have to speak with her best friends each day, consult about every clothing or household purchase, and go to almost every social event with a friend. In short, she was repeating the pattern that had characterized her relationship with her mother.

It's important to be careful when you try to move out of a smothering family relationship. Don't make a sudden break and plunge into a new involvement with peers that simply replays those old habits and behaviors. Instead, your new friendships should involve people with whom you relate on a less dependent and more equal, adult basis than you did with your mother or father.

It doesn't take more than one, two, or at the most three people for you to develop genuine friendships of the type that I'm talking about. But to build such relationships, it is necessary to spend time with these people in social encounters, long, intimate discussions, and other such contacts. These should be the sort of people whom you feel comfortable calling about matters that you might have discussed with your mother or father. When you find yourself establishing mutually interdependent ties with peers, instead of maintaining a dependent relationship with your parents, for discussion and support about deep needs and concerns, you'll know that you're well on the road to becoming your own person—apart from Mom and Dad.

## Rule #6: Tell Yourself, "I Can"

The typical image of the devoted family is one where there is a great deal of support and concern for family members. Unfortunately, though, many children of these families come away with the message, "You *can't* do it," rather than, "You *can*." Why should this be?

One reason is that children from many devoted families have had so many things done for them that they begin to feel that perhaps they really can't do certain jobs by themselves. Overly helpful moms may frequently tell a child, "You can't do that," or "Let me take care of that for you." The youngster hears these negatives so often that he or she really begins to believe them. A number of young women I've seen from enmeshed families have been told, either subtly or directly, that they really can't do anything right. Often fathers make this mistake.

One young college graduate, for example, decided to enter a vocational school because her father had drummed into her the idea that she couldn't get a management position with any company. Another young woman, though naturally intelligent and creative, had been told by her father on a regular basis, "Well, if that's the best you can do, I guess it's okay." As a result, she began to feel incompetent to do any job very well.

Nor are girls the only targets of family negativism. A young man stopped bringing his girlfriends home because every one he did introduce to his parents was criticized for one thing or another. Finally, he figured that he would never be able to choose an acceptable mate. He eventually just stopped looking for a wife.

In each of these cases, I've told the adult children to "change their tapes." By this, I mean that they tend to play old messages that they've heard from their parents over and over again in their heads. Even when their parents may not be around to say the words, the children repeat them from memory to themselves. These messages may be "You can't do it!" Or "Watch out! You'll get hurt!" Or "Oh, no, you've done it again!"

Sometimes, these "tapes" of our parents' words play so clearly in our minds that we're completely aware of what we're hearing. On other occasions, the tapes may be subconscious: The message is there, but we're not even quite aware of what is being said to us.

The taped messages that play regularly in our minds have the negative effect of keeping us from growing into independent, competent people. They are one of the major factors that can keep any dependent child from a devoted family from truly growing up.

These messages can be changed! As adults, we need to build our own tapes and then talk to ourselves over and over again with "can" messages rather than listen continually to those old "can't" tapes.

How do you change those inner tapes?

First, *listen* to that old tape. What exactly does it say? It may take a little soul-searching to discover the messages, but they'll come through if you focus on your daily attitudes toward yourself and your natural first reactions to things.

For example, what first comes into your mind when you confront a new task? Do you usually catalog the negative, difficult aspects of the job? Perhaps you conclude: "I can't do this! It's impossible!" Or when you meet a new person, do you automatically wonder what this person is finding wrong with you? You may say to yourself, "These clothes aren't right!" Or maybe, "What am I supposed to say to him?"

Once you've identified those old tapes and sorted out the negatives that you want to change, you're halfway to a solution of your problem. The next step is to make a new tape that you can play. When confronting the new task, you may make a new tape that says: "This is a challenge! I'm looking forward to learning some new things here!" Or when you meet a new person, your new tape may repeat your positive qualities and your hopes for a relationship.

Another common example of a problem that many people have with their inner tapes concerns their basic attitudes toward life when they wake up in the morning. When you roll out of bed, you may usually find yourself thinking, "Oh, no, another day of work!" Or, "How many more days to the weekend?" Or, "I've got too much to handle today!"

To change such tapes, you might instead try focusing on some new messages that go like this: "There are a lot of challenges and opportunities for me today!" Or, "I've got a lot to do, but when I take things step by step, everything always manages to get done!" From a position of faith, King David's "tape" from Psalms 118 is a great one to play first thing in the morning: "This is the day which the Lord hath made. Let us rejoice and be glad in it!"

Once you've made your new tape, play it over repeatedly in your head so that the fresh, positive message becomes familiar. Then, try to catch yourself when the old tapes begin to intrude, as they surely will at various times. When they do, consciously turn off those old messages and turn on the new ones!

One young woman who came to me for help had a persistent, terrible tape playing in her head as a result of her relationship with her mother. She had absorbed the idea that it was up to her to make up for everything that her father, her brothers, and her sisters had not done for her mother. Yet she always felt she was never really living up to her mother's expectations. She regularly thought, "I have to call mother. I need to be with her. I'd better see if she needs anything."

As a result of our discussions, she finally settled on a new tape that she began to repeat to herself. This new, more constructive message went something like this: "I can't be my mother's mate, and I can't be her parent. No child can be. The best way that I can help my mother is to become strong myself. The more independent I am, the more I'll be able to relate to my mother as an adult and be one child she is proud of."

Think again about what is on those old tapes in your mind. Evaluate just how accurate they are. Then, make a new tape to substitute for the old, childhood messages.

Begin to repeat that new, positive, adult message on a regular basis, and especially when you catch the old tape coming on.

Keep it fairly simple and, if possible, catchy. That way, you'll be able to remember it easily, and it will be more likely to perk you up. One man I know settled on that line from the children's story, *The Little Engine That Could*: "I think I can, I think I can, I think I can. I thought I could. . . ." As you'll probably recall, this little engine managed to climb a seemingly insuperable mountain just because it believed that it could accomplish the task!

The nice thing about following these rules for growing is that the more you follow them, the more you grow, the more you become independent and competent. You already have an extremely strong base—strong "roots," as we have called them—because your family has given you a great deal of love, support, and acceptance. Now, you need to use those roots. It's time to begin to grow to new levels of personal success and satisfaction.

With your new capacity for growth, you'll find that it's no longer necessary to be held back by the Dependent Love Pattern. It's no longer necessary to be locked into a love–hate relationship with your mother, or a distant, unsatisfying relationship with your father. Nor is it inevitable that you have to experience less-than-fulfilling relationships with your spouse or friends.

In short, the way is now open for you to enjoy true love and genuine adult relationships. It's time for you to grow!

# Afterword

By now, you probably realize that although your feelings often center on one person—such as a love–hate attitude toward your mother—those feelings are actually symptoms of a much larger family pattern. You've begun to look at your own family more closely, and gradually you're coming to a better understanding of your family and yourself.

When you come from a close, devoted family, it's sometimes hard to loosen up, to let go and work toward change. The most important value in your family is to stay together, and the greatest fear is endangering that closeness and caring. It's terribly difficult to take steps toward independence. It's hard to believe that in the painful process of letting go, things are actually going to get better. But paradoxically, beneficial transformation is often just what happens.

As I have watched devoted families change, I have seen them begin to spend less time together but enjoy the time they do share even more. I see that they often talk less frequently and for less time, but they are more genuine and caring when they do talk. I see family members disagreeing more, but fighting less.

When relationships are so close as to stifle individuality, or when a parent does so much for a child that the child doesn't learn to do for himself, tension and even hatred can arise. Fights can become the principal means of asserting individuality. If appropriate limits and roles can be established, a more genuine adult closeness will be the result.

For devoted families, change must come in the encouragement of more independence. The ultimate goal in striving toward independence is not individual autonomy, but healthy relationships. Relationships become stronger as we correct imbalances. So our goal is genuine, adult relationships with the people who mean the most to us—our families and our friends.

What does genuine adult closeness look like? There's a balance between accepting that each person is different, and acknowledging caring and interdependence. One person must be able to disagree with another without posing any threat. Then, when an agreement is reached, everyone will understand it's genuine and not the product of fear or unhealthy compliance. In addition to becoming independent, mature adults can show care without any fear of being "absorbed" or overwhelmed by the person who is the recipient of their concern.

Sometimes, of course, people feel discouraged with the process of change. When two steps forward are followed by one step backward, the overall progress may be hard to see. What sounds like a simple task in the counseling office may be extremely difficult to execute with real family members. A simple, small change may seem enormous against the weight of family habits and routines.

In these circumstances, grand goals may be beyond comprehension. Yet just as a small pebble thrown into the water causes gradually widening ripples, so too, even small changes in a family may set off a new and exciting pattern that can have wide-ranging effects on relationships.

Often, people I've worked with return to see me thoroughly excited about the positive changes they have experienced. A son came in, still surprised that his quiet father had actually responded with understanding when he had finally shared his sexual struggles. A mother was amazed that her daughter, who had always refused to do tasks about the house, actually showed a significant increase in self-confidence after she was required to assume certain responsibilities. Some parents who began to work on their marital conflicts were gratified to see their children's problems simultaneously resolving themselves.

Of all the families I've worked with, the Devoted Families have made the biggest changes most easily. A key reason for their success is that, even towards their problems, they demonstrate a persistent caring and commitment that is so critical for lasting growth.

# Index

# About the Author

Anne F. Grizzle is a psychotherapist in New York City, specializing in family therapy and family development seminars. She serves as a counselor at the First Presbyterian Church in Flushing and as a trainer for the Counseling Resource Center in Manhattan. Previously, Ms. Grizzle worked as a therapist at the Foundation for Depression and Manic Depression and as a supervisor and training coordinator for the New York Foundling Hospital. Ms. Grizzle obtained her B.A. in psychology and social relations from Harvard University, her M.S. in social work from Columbia University, and a certificate in advanced family therapy from Hunter College, City University of New York. Currently, Ms. Grizzle resides with her husband and two sons in New York.